PAUL CHAT … OUD

The Eye of the Ventriloquist

to Aoibheann
and Ömndar
You will find a lot of thing
about the green gate and Donegal
But a lot lot more about life, love
and everything.
A very big kiss

4th August 10

Les cygnes

Original title: Le regard du ventriloque.

Translated from the French by Allaye O'Connor,
with full verification and approval from the author.

With many thanks to Sarah Harrison
for her invaluable suggestions.

Editorial adviser : Monique de Montremy
Cover design by Jean-Hugues Bancaud

Baghdad 2003 by Don McCullin, photographer.
« The greatest British photographer of the 20th century »
The *Independent* - London.

The future is in books

For Paul Chatenoud
for your kindness.
with respect and best
wishes
Don.

photograph by DON McCULLIN

Foreword

My aim in writing this book is to try to uncover that hidden element of those things which fill our lives. That part we neither care nor wish to see. So open your eyes wide as I take you to the very core of my fantasies, utopias and dreams, without which nothing of any lasting effect is achieved in this world. To bury one's imagination is the hardest thing to bear, so continue to believe in miracles: for I have truly experienced them.

The anecdotes herein, whether real or imagined, serve only to convey with more force both my philosophy and perception of life.

Press Advance

Before this book was published a number of newspapers (including The *Sunday Times*, *Le Monde* and The *Financial Times*) had already mentioned that the work was in progress. It was also featured in a BBC interview expressing interest in the content. I hope that the completed work leaves none disappointed.

Acknowledgments

To all those wanderers;
Homer, first among them
Montaigne, who roamed the spirit
Freud, wanderer of the soul
Proust, whose sentences roamed
Panait Istrati, most brilliant roamer of all
Lacan, and his roaming brilliance
Brassens and his roving heart
All of whom
Helped me stay on my feet
And showed me
The path of the wandering life.

To my son, Edouard,

who urged me to set down these “crazy memoirs”.

He’ll get what he asked for!

Prologue

I may as well start at the very beginning: I lost my mother when I was two and a half years old. Of course I'm not the only one to have experienced this. The event has had major repercussions throughout my life. My mother lies in the cemetery of a small town near Casablanca. Every time I visit this part of the world, I never fail to go and pay my respects.

On my last trip to this realm, I naturally made my customary pilgrimage. In spite of the many years that had passed, as I approached the little town, I was overwhelmed with emotion when I remembered how, as children, then adolescents, my father led us every first of November to the cemetery where we would place chrysanthemums on her grave.

My emotion increased as I caught sight of the trees around the cemetery. Then came a terrible shock. As I passed through the gate I saw youngsters playing football on a perfectly mowed pitch. My emotion gave way to a sort of unutterable emptiness. I was quite incapable of reconciling the two places in my mind (no doubt because I've never liked football).

I made my way to the French embassy and they solved the mystery for me. The chargé d'affaires, who received me with utmost courtesy, explained that the town had wanted to reclaim the site and so the few remaining French citizens buried there had been removed to Casablanca. To emphasize his sincerity and the seamless workings of French administration, he showed me the exhumation file. I had no memory of how my mother looked and yet now, here I was confronted by a photograph of a transparent bag bearing her name and through which could be seen her remains. The clerk was perplexed by my confusion. The poor man could hardly have known that I had never consciously seen my mother, neither in the flesh nor "in the bones". As I returned home to friends that evening, I was able to proudly tell them: "Well, I lost my mother, but now I have found her again."

The Eye of the Ventriloquist

(A necessary diatribe)*

For several decades I have roamed this earth. I should say a handful of decades, for I am nearly at the age when Casanova withdrew from life in order to write the story of his former conquests. This is not my case. My loves are still alive and I have no need of the Chateau de Dux to live my life to the full. Instead, it continues to unfold like a carpet, reddened by the fuchsia petals which lie strewn on the lane leading up to my cottage in Ireland from where I look down on the ocean.

It was Proust who led me here, quite some time ago. I was 25, lying on a beach in Corsica next to a girl in full bloom, reading *In Search of…* when I came across this sentence: "Before knowing solitude, all we are concerned with is knowing in what measure we might reconcile it with certain pleasures, which cease to be such, as soon as we have experienced it." This sentence has been my guiding light until this day.

I chose Ireland because I understood perfectly what Eamon de Valera [1] had expressed in one sentence: "The Irish genius has always placed spiritual and intellectual values above material ones." Alas, this is no longer true today. The American sirens are quashing the Irish spirit, as they continue to do everywhere else in the world.

**(Diatribe: criticism relying heavily on indignation, irony and derision)* Epictetus.

Ulysses, where are you?
With Kazantzaki, feasting far from Ithaca?
With Joyce, lost in the Dedalus of Dublin?
Or with Brassens, lost in suburbia? [2]

Here, firmly anchored to my hill, I stand fast. Far from the media whirl, I nevertheless find myself at the centre of all these currents through the guests whom I receive and who are themselves immersed in either the political, artistic or financial lives of their respective countries. It is through them and because of my geographical position that I have an instant overview of the events and arcane mysteries of politics which preoccupy them, intimacies which both this place and my own curious nature invite.

Unfortunately, I dithered around for a long time before finally settling down. It has to be said that Mercury had me take his winged rod for a ship's anchor. It took me some time to realise my mistake and for years I continued to follow the endless twists and turns in the rope which would lead me to that anchor which I so coveted.

Now that the anchor is well and truly cast, and in spite of the shifting sands which surround it, I can take stock. The other day, coming down from the sodden hill, carefully avoiding the clods of earth and stones that a recent storm had brought down, I came to Maghera beach, sparkling with a superb pallor in this incredible place. It was then that some verses that I had composed on this same spot in Donegal, more than twenty years ago, came back to me:

May the distant stars continue along their path
May tears fall on stones
May the mistral blow in the Ardennes
    A child quivers as he clutches his copybook
    Which would rather sound the alarm
    Thus changing the course of his heavenly vision

When the crazed red stars continue to sound
When tears burst asunder the stones on the road
When the Ardennes march on to Deauville
        An adolescent comes slowly down from the stars
        And points his feverish and hesitant finger
        Toward a long swathe of hair bearing eyes of fate
How the wheel crushes the Milky Way
How the tears so extracted sparkle like stars
How Deauville on the strand became Blonville
        A man advances steadily
        Straddling with certainty
        All of his past
Why destiny so unsmiling and infallible
Why these useless tears burst into diamonds
Why would Blonville come forth from your white robe.

I continued along my path, for want of anything better, towards the vast, deserted, shivering beach, and these few verses which would not detach themselves from the white sand. Unconsciously, my pen had traced these sentences whose hidden power I had not suspected at the time; which is perhaps the boldest example of poetry. Socrates knew that he didn't know. I myself knew, but I didn't know what. Now that I know that I know, I still have to put it into words. Today, in spite of the wind which had stiffened considerably, and the white sand which stung my face, I understood the meaning of my lines better. I hastened my steps to return home, as the November days were drawing in. I could smell the scent of the turf fire caught on the wind, long before I saw the smoke coming from my chimney, transforming the cottage into a sort of stationary locomotive, almost unreal as it sat swathed in its gaspings. A long night awaited me. Alone. Wrapped in the sound and the mists of the ocean. Alone? No. There was the persistent thump of the poem which gave me goose bumps even more than the quickening wind. The same wind which might tear down a few clumps of thatch in the night, yet I had nothing to fear. The preceding week Malachy had reinforced the ropes which held down the rushes on the thatched roof. The wind grew stronger. I summoned up all sorts of ruses to muster courage and remain calm. What could possibly happen to me? Memories of sailing the stormy seas? Yes, of course. But looking back these memories were not so dangerous; others were far more insidious and more subtly undermining. From time to time I listened to the opera for which Hermann had drawn inspiration from *Wuthering Heights*, and that evening Cathy's air came back full pelt. The long swathe of hair bearing eyes of fate thus re-emerged. Having pinpointed my anxiety, I at last fell peacefully asleep. The next day a soothing wind blew steadily. The clouds had been blown away to reveal an incredibly blue sky which appeared to spill over the horizon into the far beyond, into the future. The future, which of course you already know. I too know it well. I know it better than anything, for it stems from infancy. From childhood to the grave, it's just a matter of buttocks; soft, plump bottoms that we cover with talcum powder, or wrinkled ones that we hide. Between the two, that strife of every human being to feel the thrill just a little more, to fill up the daily grind with far-flung dreams and to fall anew, ingloriously, one's heart exposed.

Here, things are different; the Irish like to talk in proverbs, such as: "things are terrible but it doesn't matter". One sentence reaches you and the world becomes humane again. Just for a moment, until memories of times past catch up with you once more.

Like that Christmas eve when a neighbour climbed the long drive through the rain and the dark to bring the solitary 'Frenchman' a Christmas cake that she had made especially for him. I still remember her two outstretched hands bearing the offering, reaching out before a soaked figure lit up by an enormous smile. This scene remains engraved on my mind along with its smaller sister which occurred in the Moroccan desert: from nowhere 'a blue man' made the same elegant gesture offering me some *kessera* which he had just cooked – the same wide smile bestowed on the stranger who was passing along 'his road'.

In every corner of the world, it is the people of little means who are ready to give what little they have. As for the others, those 'good' folk, those who have many things, they would never make such an elegant gesture, for they are far too frightened of not having enough. They do not know what they are missing; the very heartbeat of life itself.

In order to immerse myself more fully in the Irish spirit, I decided to learn the language of this land. No doubt, in order to better understand the Irish people. Probably in order to understand their culture. No doubt, also from a linguistic love of language. Not least of all, the guilty feeling I had retained of never having learnt Arabic during my childhood in Morocco. Perhaps, too, in order to be able to read the signs and signposts. In order to shine in company, to my detriment, for Irish Gaelic is not an easy language to master.

The Roman ratio never invaded the shores of Hibernia and if Saint Patrick succeeded where Caesar had failed, then this demonstrates that the Celts are simply more susceptible to the Curia than to being crushed. The English know something of this.

I was more amused than surprised by my linguistic discoveries. Notably by the fact that '*cailín*' (pronounced as the French 'câline') means 'girl', but is a masculine noun, and '*stail*' which means 'stallion', is feminine. Of course the fact that stallion should be feminine immediately put a clamp on the Gallic cock's beak, whereas the fact that *cailín* was masculine left me all admiration. It's their way of acknowledging feminine might. Something obvious, which we should recall from time to time: every macho, the apparent epitome of power, is reduced to a quivering heap before the greatest of all adoring creatures – the Mother. But this is exactly where the plot thickens. Eager to display my knowledge to the Gaelic Mothers, I received a stinging and even aggressive rebuke. Wanting to prove my sincerity, I heard myself say "Your books are wrong, Sir". With all flags flying, I had brandished the feminist standard: a crude blunder that the Mamas would never forgive. Feminine might cannot be seen to be fluttering in the wind. For that you have the ventriloquist's word. Proof, were it needed, that learning a language doesn't make you more intelligent. I, who had learnt German and Italian in order to sing opera, had never doubted this.

The sun had not yet decided to set and me neither. So I took the path which led to the beach. From a neighbouring field old Sean greeted me with the timeless "soft day". His donkey was pulling a bundle of hay which slid over the grass. All winter long, this was the only man I saw, sometimes from a long way off. He didn't even have a cart to take the hay to his cows.

My footsteps marked the white beach as though to contest refusal. But this undeniable proof of my passing was not enough. It takes more than a few pieces of evidence, however sound, to prevent denial from rearing its head. Before my eyes the sea continued to fold the solid scattered rocks beneath its successive waves until they disappeared under the rising tide. There seemed to be an enveloping tide in the Mamas' refusal. I resolved to no longer query the Irish Mamas regarding the gender of their daughters.

From the depths of the love of my life
Rises a desire from time beyond time
Which warms my heart so frighted

That dizzying fear shrouded in a gratuitous gesture
That which does not consume the soul.
Along the twists and turns of your stunning insouciance
The old doctor has passed away
And your distant outline moves me still
Should you cry in spite of the lantern

Take arms against these glittering rags
And take down from their frozen pedestal those gaudy decorations.
Behind the two-way mirror
Perhaps an unadorned woman
Who could become your light.
Breaking through the storms
We are sometimes dazzled
It's the price we pay to stay on course.

My outpourings were halted by two girls bursting with youth whom I spied from my window. Rushing down the neighbouring field, their piercing laughter evoked neither love, sensuality nor desire. A recent, rather intangible passion, had quenched my fervour. The king of disasters had been pushed back a little further. The star had gone off course and fallen near where it came down, as soldiers say of the wasted bullet.

I finished my honeymoon in reverse order. She had said to me "I'm glad I know you". This idiot really believed she did. Then she added: "I can't see you, I just see your soul." What do you do with a body buried under a soul? Deploy one's humour in order to contest the wild imaginings which fissure, in every sense, my jointed façade. I was floating in the mists, hovering above the sands, like an African mirage. Your daring expression said: "You are the sun which dazzles my life and brings light to my bed." Alas, I was just a fragment of a lost star drifting on a path which you sought to understand.

To be in love is to love the changing reflections of a star which we imagine we possess wholly, able to change its path. Just one definition of love among so many.

I had managed several times over to leave the course that the great '*cailín*' had wanted to map out for me. Like the English woman, whom I congratulated upon her husband's appointment as head of a large international company and who replied to me on the telephone: "Paul, if you had wanted to be that director, you would have been." The silence which followed my explosion of laughter revealed her continuing incomprehension. Some years later I did not congratulate her when he was knighted. This time I burst out laughing at the thought of kneeling down before Her Majesty or addressing the formulaic letter of thanks: "I am honoured to be Your Majesty's humble and obedient subject." How could one do such a thing, I said to myself. A few months ago I received a note from a castle in Scotland where this beauty had withdrawn with her knighted director: "Paul, you were right."

I very much like the English expression 'at the end of the day'. While waiting for the end of the day, how many lives have been wasted by this quest for recognition? The craving for social promotion is the same sort of thing. As an Irish friend said to me, put a donkey in a lift and he'll go up! You find them on every floor.

Sometimes I think back to the old cottage I rented when I arrived in Ireland. Situated a hundred metres from the ocean, the salt air ate away at everything. I had come to rebuild the world and all I did was repaint things. I tried to rationalize my manual endeavours with a sentence from Gustave Mahler: "That which we create is of mere passing importance. What man makes of himself through his constant labour, this is what really lasts. What we leave behind us is simply the skin, the casing. *The Master Singers,* the *Ninth, Faust,* all these things are but skins shed." [3]

This weighting of Mahler's reflections in favour of my handiwork, was of no great comfort to me. I'd as well tell myself over and again: it doesn't matter what you do, it's what you become through doing it. It didn't really work out that way.

A few years later I saw the cottage again: overgrown by briars and plants the thatch roof had collapsed! (My ex-wife, who had come to see me with some friends, said to them: "and when I think that he left me for *that*". The work that I had done "my shed skin", had well and truly fallen down… and the *Ninth* was floating high in the European skies.

The dream of creation. The dreams we build for ourselves. The secret dream and the creature of our dreams whose look we never forget. The mane of hair bearing the eyes of destiny, once again. I was struggling with the reality of my fantasies, as the December sun actually warmed my hand through the window. A nearby calf that had just been separated from its mother, was mooing with all its might. I'd as well tell him it would pass, he would never have believed me. Perhaps he would have sensed that my words didn't ring true.

For a moment I thought I was in one of Ingmar Bergman's black and white films. The sea was as black as the clouds which tried in vain to find their reflection therein. The foam, which was as white as the hungry seagulls, was lifted from the tips of the waves by sharp gusts of wind. Yet the reddened eyes, no doubt moistened by the salt spray, were real enough. They were following a funeral procession as far as the small church made of black stone. The red beard in the coffin belonged to a young man. He had just discovered that his sister was his mother… He had killed himself. The slimy water of the bog had swallowed up his body, stripped of the murky origins of this revelation. The deep purple fuchsias, the mauve heather, the beech trees, and the love-lies-bleeding, fed back their primal colours to this deathly amniotic fluid. His clothes, hung on a tree like Christ on the cross, bore witness to his sufferings. What else can one do with a fate which seems so dark.

As in the Mediterranean regions, where only the men were seated for the meal which followed, the great '*cailíns*' are there to feed their grown-up children who are going to die. That evening, the presence of a rat gnawing away in the rafters seemed of more solace than that of a king in the depths of my solitude.

Occasionally during those long evenings, I bade the rat take audience of my outpourings. I thought I would thus escape the fate of those people who watch themselves speak, as others listen to themselves, mimicry gaining over intonation. Nothing could be further from the truth. On the contrary, I was able to combine the two: with my hand extended and vengeful finger, intoning loudly, I thus astonished an imaginary audience with my performance. As for my rat, that mangy animal from the sod, he acquired the status of a high-minded audience all of his own. Yet none was fooled, except perhaps the spiders that paused for a while. The reality of my existence seemed to hang from a thread, the very one that made up the spider's web.

At times, this thread which you grip and which holds you, has to be invented. Just like that old and lonely Parisian woman who invented friends for herself. She used to send herself postcards which, as they arrived before the caretaker's astonished eyes via her lodge, symbolised her existence. Someone, somewhere, had not forgotten her. Furthermore, claiming that she never kept them, she went even further in her private subterfuge, by giving them to the gossipy caretaker who decorated her humble abode with sunny beaches… This performance put the old woman on an equal footing with the other tenants who had gone on holiday. As she struggled from day to day, this fictitious array of images eased her childish heart.

Since then, without worrying about the faintly ridiculous aspect of this ritual, which used to annoy me so much, I have sent postcards to old ladies.

Of course, within the endless range of pipe dreams, one can find better. Even more adulatory than a rat, more unappetizing than a spider and more exalting than the wonderment of one's caretaker. If a child needs the mirror of his parents in order to develop, the adult needs the twinkle from some plaything. Even though the choice of some of these sometimes seems pathetic, I still see why they are needed. Without the bleep of its radar beacons, a boat would be nothing but an awkward bladder, tossed from one side to the other on its journey. In the cove below some young surfers were moving gracefully around the buoys which they had set in a line for the purpose of their game. Occasionally, after suddenly falling into the water, they used the buoys to catch their breath again. I too had tried to surf through life, attempting to avoid those boundaries which society had imposed on me. Then those old pillars in the shifting silt had proved themselves helpful. My dusty star was now bouncing off the lights from those playthings. I clung to the reminders and childhood dreams as though to a lifebuoy.

That afternoon, as I collected the broken branches brought down by the storm into the lane, I was not surprised to see spiders webs still intact and shining brilliantly. I felt reassured by my fantasies, just as Casanova had done by the magic circle that he himself designed as a means of seduction. The magical power of his conviction had protected him from the rumblings of the storm within the circle that he had invented. Those fantasies, those imaginings, are the crutches which have helped me to fulfill my dreams.

As a young man, an English friend asked me at the time whether, being single, I had found "my Waterloo". As a Frenchman, I replied that I hoped I would never find her. Even though Austerlitz may also lead to Saint Helena.

Saint Helena, Saint Helena, dreary island whose child king had always fascinated me by his endless search for the maternal love he would never find. James Sant's portrait of him captures this in an extraordinary way. In the heavy unspoken expression, there arises the unattainable conquest of a kingdom of love, alongside which the memory of the flashing imperial crown appears dull.

I was fourteen when, browsing through an historical review, I was literally struck by the obsessive melancholia in the bitter expression of the ventriloquist. Since that time, this portrait has never left me. Fifty years later it still graces my library, here in Ireland. The sad and powerful expression had been with me for so long that, while on a journey to Scotland, I decided to go and see the original painting. The French Consulate of Saint Helena had informed me that it was to be found in the museum in Glasgow. It was not on view. I managed to convince the curator to take me to their store room. Words cannot describe my disappointment when my eyes fell on the pale washed pink cheeks and the grim look of the declining Emperor. Who was the artist? The photographer, who, making good use of the shadows had captured the essence of the original? The painter who had given expression to that essence? Or myself, who had seen within it that which I had wanted to see: the eye of the ventriloquist.

This portrait still intrigues the Irish people who penetrate my lair; by this I mean my library crammed with books up to the ceiling, but the ceiling is very low. This detail is important, because it allows me to avoid the fate of Charles Valentin Alcan who, wishing to take a book from the top of his bookshelves, was killed as the latter collapsed on him. Books are very dangerous, they can kill. Certain people, on seeing this portrait, think that I adhere to a cult of the Emperor. The unsayable being impossible to talk about, I let them say what they wish. Yet it is thanks to this portrait that I learnt that it was the Irish who had made a cult of him: there are more than a hundred traditional ballads in his honour, like this one :

"We waited in vain for the French to arrive
But Bony set sail with his army for Egypt
But if he should still come, we'll be there for to meet him
And all will be ready for to join his command,
And we'll march out like heroes with our green banners flying
And Napoleon would have been there in the van." [4]

Napoleon is said to have written: "If I had ventured over to Ireland instead of Egypt in 1798, where would England and indeed the world, be now?"

A journalist from *The Daily Telegraph* used this story to promote the B&B that I had just created with these words: "Napoleon never came to Ireland, Paul Chatenoud did. He came, he saw, and with his inimitable, subversive humour, he conquered." My ego, used to another kind of conquest, suffered something of a blow. Never mind, you have to carry the eye of the ventriloquist to the very end. (*The Daily Telegraph*, 5th January 2002) [5]

This morning my rather dark mood left me thinking about things past. As a young man, the death of Che Guevara had made my blood boil. As a Frenchman and Parisian, I somewhat regretted that no struggle had been required in order to enjoy the freedom that others had won for me. Even the fight to dress as we wished no longer meant anything. The Beatnik fashion held no sway with my generation. It meant something across the Atlantic, the Channel and the Rhine. On the banks of the Seine, the young people decked out in this regalia were mostly foreigners. They had come to show their freedom at little cost: the restraining yokes were a little less rigid here. At times a mocking smile greeted them. As was the case one evening in a bar where the élite of Saint-Germain-des-Prés tended to congregate. A young American, dressed in the Beatnik style, walked across the room. There was a condescending smile on everyone's lips. The young man stopped, took a lighter out of his pocket and lit a cigarette that an attractive young woman had just taken out of a packet. Boris Vian would have liked the irony of this homage to his widow. [6]

Today, decades later, Che Guevara remains dead. His image can still be found on postcards and T-shirts. The countryfolk of Higuera who denounced him to the soldiers are still alive. Their hair has whitened, but above all it's their betrayal which they have sanitised by sanctifying "*el commandante*". He has become the person whom the mothers pray to for help with difficult births; he who wanted to be the midwife of a better world. Yet there remains a faint glow of hope. That which we perceive on certain evenings in the rocky terrain of the rio Yuro. A few votive candles sparingly placed remind us of Che's last battle. This little glow of hope is the one which often highlights those causes we believe to have been lost. In the minds of many people it is often the winner's name that is forgotten.

Daddy's world will always have to be made over again, Mummy's wardrobe too. We believe we can recreate the world by launching a new fashion in the name of freedom. But freedom is neither simply a matter of dress, nor of being part of a crowd, nor of a second coming. Here in Ireland, it is the muse which gives expression to the irrepressibly libertarian soul of the Celtic people, a spirit which centuries of religion have not succeeded in repressing. I too considered myself a Celtic spirit. But my Cartesian mind would resist this for a long time yet. It took me more than forty years to free myself from the yoke of religion weighing upon me since childhood. I was helped by an inherited lucidity. At times this very lucidity prevented all action. But then life would carry me on, and knowing all the risks, I built my house on sand. Even though it is incurable, I know what I'm doing and don't give a damn. Except when I roam; then my lucidity always precedes me and, sometimes, it gets in the way.

In May 68, it was this same lucidity that prevented me from fully engaging in the movement. Although I felt sympathy for anything that might break a few chains, I could not bring myself to throw the derisory paving stone and take part in the revolution. At the time I had a student job which involved driving people home from a well-known establishment in an old English taxi. This incongruous vehicle allowed me to cross both the police blockades and student line without a hitch. The astonishment which the car aroused served as a permit. A film-maker friend used the car in order to capture scenes from both sides. One evening, without the protection of this magic car, I sought to get a little closer. Suitably attired, I walked alongside the CRS buses parked on the Boulevard Saint-Germain, when a CRS policeman, frustrated at not being able to do anything and seeing a head passing directly below him, immediately made use of his baton. The resulting lump was the only wound that I sustained during those eventful days. The only mention that I received was from a fashionable singer of the time whom I drove one warm evening along the back streets of Saint-Germain. She insulted the police through the rear window and dedicated her last album with these words : "To Paul, in memory of the revolution!!!"

Some people are surprised that a number of the leading lights of May 68 were the sons of bourgeois families. From Spartacus to Marx, not forgetting Talleyrand, history has taught us that very often, in order to find its voice, a revolution needs class transgressors. One cannot really reproach the leaders of May 68 for being from bourgeois backgrounds, since this was a *sine qua non*. One can merely confirm that they remained upper class, and that their search for power remained unchanged.

This was not my only claim to fame. On one other occasion, much later on, I was travelling to Madrid. The plane had been overbooked and the airline company had offered me a first-class seat. The forty-something, well-dressed and greying man whom I found myself next to, engaged me in conversation. He had spent four years in one of Pinochet's prisons. "My body is covered in scars. It has been branded by torturers assigned to prison holes where there was no law. I became a shapeless heap, shoved from one uniform into another and branded with a red hot iron."

- What are you doing now with that legacy of suffering? was the only reply that I could formulate.
- These days I'm involved in the revolution in Central America. I go round the European capitals in order to raise money for Nicaragua. Yesterday I was in Paris, where all those involved in the war were meeting secretly to see whether or not a cease-fire was possible. We quickly reached an agreement: there was no point in stopping the war. That would simply deprive us of all the financial help that we were getting. France has just accorded us a state-of-the-art military hospital. Without the war we would never have got it.

The logic behind his reasoning was implacable. I gave him a few lines from my own life - that I lived in Ireland and prided myself on the fact that I wrote.

"A French intellectual who lives in Ireland, that could only be in order to assist the Irish revolutionary cause," he cried peremptorily.

Try as I might to dissuade him, he would have none of it.

"You are wasting your time over there; come and join us, we need people like you," the Chilean insisted as he handed me his card, which bore the address of the most illustrious Parisian hotel at that time.

I always found it difficult to accommodate grand revolutionary ideals with the very sinews of war: money. That day I had been mistaken for a revolutionary, no doubt because I was travelling first class. I had become a class transgressor in a back-to-front way.

Today, years later, I could say to my Chilean acquaintance: history is obstinate, it will remember Mr Kissinger's 1973 11th September before the other one. To crush a democracy is a crime against humanity, to crush two tower blocks is a crime against men. Yet history is generous too, it will leave Mr Kissinger to fall into the common grave, whereas Pablo Neruda will shine for the common cause. For the second anniversary of the collapse of the twin towers, *Le Monde* published a very provocative drawing by the illustrator Plantu: it features a US Air Force plane about to crash into two towers representing Chile. It says everything. [7]

There is one man that not even the wind blowing between the two towers could bring down. He was the young Frenchman who, with the aid of a bow, suspended a steel wire between the two towers in the 1970s. Eight times over he set out across this wire with his balancing pole. On the ground below the anxious spectators were watching for the mistake which would bring about his fall. But it was not he that fell.

I sometimes think about the pilots who flew into the two towers. Of course they may be in heaven surrounded by seventy-two virgins, but I am not so sure. Whereas the thirty thousand Argentinian suspects thrown from planes were accompanied by priests in order to exonerate the soldiers. Perhaps the idea of falling to earth from a very great height was aimed at bringing them closer to *the* Great Height. Amongst those who lived through the collapse of the towers, there are those who will never return. Then there are those of whom it is said they never got over it: one person couldn't believe his eyes when he was offered a free coffee, the other because he wasn't made to pay for his telephone call. The collapse of the towers was in fact overshadowed in their minds by these two gestures which were so out of the ordinary. A third person went down to smoke a cigarette. Let it never be said that it was a cigarette that saved his life.

Nowadays smoking has become the hidden enemy of all those sticklers, moralists, pompous doctors and every kind of proselytising lecturer which are sprouting up everywhere at the moment. In times gone by they were called sanctimonious prigs. As religion has advanced, they are now known as *ayatollahs*. If Ireland was the first European member state to enforce the no-smoking ban, it shouldn't be forgotten that until recently it was also the most God-fearing country of our continent. An Irish friend whom I asked whether the Irish still believed in God, replied: "In God, I don't know, but in religion definitely." I was going to say thanks be to God, the Church has gone into freefall these past few years.

During the last century it was the Church which tried to dictate to us how we might love by castigating the notion of sex. Fortunately for us poor sinners, medicine and politics, along with smoking, have become greater topics of interest. Medicine, for the obvious reason that reassurance must be brought to the might of its profession (the 39% of doctors and 43% of nurses who smoke are either played down or dismissed on grounds of human imperfection). As for politicians, they need to reaffirm a crumbling majority. It is interesting to note that it was in Ireland that people came out and demonstrated on the greatest scale against the war in Iraq. (Buses bound for Dublin set out from every village). The agreement which gave the Americans the right to use Shannon airport was not welcomed by the majority of Irish people. (Thereby effectively became in law and in deed aiders and abettors of the invasion of Iraq). Realising that 70% of their electorate were non-smokers, the government decided to pass an anti-smoking law which would allow a return to favour: "Look at the great government we've got, it's keeping an eye on our health."

Other governments who were aping the American way of life followed suit. In fact, what appeared under the guise of public health concerns, was the reappearance of the old moral order: It's bad, we've got to protect our children, etc. Just as masturbation was said to lead to deafness, now it is smoking which leaves you impotent. "Look to your soul, which should be pure and without stain, far from any thought of sex," said the Church. Now modern research tells us: "Look after your lungs which should be clean and pure, and your sexual life will be likewise." These new *ayatollahs* dressed in three-piece suits cannot stand the fact that, whatever form it may take, we might be in a state of pleasure.

Being rather badly placed on this matter, the Church itself now accepts sexual pleasure. Having always known, throughout the course of history, how to jump on board a moving train, it now feels obliged to quietly accept that smoking is also a pleasure. Take the priest in southern France who has opened his church to smokers by arranging ashtrays at the bottom of the nave. ("Smokers may now make a little prayer at the same time, since they no longer have the right to smoke in a café").

When the anti-smoking ban was being debated, I raised my voice in an article published by The *Irish Times* under 'An Irishman's Diary'. The only person to rise to my defence was a bishop who responded with an article in another newspaper [8]. To the astonishment of the chief editor there was not a single letter sent in objecting to my article!

Contrary to what we have been led to believe, this law has had its antecedents. One of the first names given to tobacco was "the holy grass". This proved unfavourable with Pope Urbain VIII who, in 1644, excommunicated smokers, calling them the new heretics. He had understood that it might induce a pleasurable sensation. But like his condemnation of Galileo, his 'smoking edict' didn't go down too well and disappeared in a puff of smoke.

Let's hope that the same will come of those laws which have arrived from across the Atlantic and which are invading Europe. The mayor of New York and his friend, Bill Gates, (who is otherwise a very generous man) have just created a $500 million dollar foundation dedicated to the eradication of tobacco on this planet. Quite apart from the fact that this money could be used for more urgent matters, it is interesting to note that they already have offices located in 179 countries. What reassures me is that this figure is still a long way from the 761 military bases (acknowledged by the Pentagon) spread across the world. The smoke from American bombs will continue to rise for some time.

Glimmers of hope begin to appear: the law has been relaxed in Greece and Spain where you may now smoke in restaurants and bars. We are going in the right direction, humanity still has a chance: in China, the new model economy, 67% of men and 50% of doctors are smokers.

It has to be said that here in Ireland, the ridiculous nature of certain regulations can only make you smile. You may smoke in your hotel room, prison cell or convent. The Church still has sufficient might to protect its smoking nuns, but a lorry driver, alone in his truck cabin, is not allowed to smoke (it's his work place). He can and must be reported (it has already happened). If you are caught smoking in a pub, you can be sent to prison where you will be allowed to smoke. Finally, the international lawyers are still battling it out to try and decide whether you can smoke on an Irish ferry vessel sailing in international waters…

Since smoking has been banned from work places, school children can now gawk at smokers puffing away for as long as they like, as they stand outside pubs and buildings. A good example for the youth of today if ever there was. I don't know if this is why in Japan it is forbidden to smoke in the street, where, on the contrary, you have to go into a bar to do so. "Truth to one side of the Pyrenees, untruth to the other…" [9]

Now let's get back to more serious matters. For some years now we should no longer have seen anyone smoking on television. Neither in films, nor during news broadcasts. And what do we see: a murder every ten minutes, in every documentary, in every film, in every news shot where mangled bodies are shown alongside smashed-up cars. But that isn't the problem. Killing isn't such a serious matter. The most important thing is that the killer is a non-smoker. The banks and the stock exchange can collapse. That's not too serious either. The important thing is that people respect the smoking ban in their offices.

Since the beginning of humanity, and throughout the world, Man has always sought to allay his existential anguish with the use of certain palliatives: alcohol, various drugs, excessive work, psychotropic medicines, ambition in politics, sport, the army, theatre, or, religious intransigence, bulimia, gambling, compulsive spending or sexuality. All in order to wipe out, for a few moments, the painful reality which surrounds us. To forget and to help the child who is still inside us and still part of us to forget the break with the ideal world. So in order to ease the blow of this break with a lost ideal world, we turn to various palliatives which assume the role of a substitute, thus making us feel that we are in control of the situation as we feel better and fulfilled. Yet at the first unexpected reappearance, whether real or imaginary, of that lost ideal world, we have to start all over again. This is why will power has absolutely no hold over the dominant childhood emotions which are still part of us. That small child has to be taken in hand, or rather by the hand and shown, by our mature self, the way along life's path. The path which, however hard we try, cannot be controlled but only accepted.

I myself have used one such palliative after another simply in order to remain upright. In childhood and in adolescence they were necessary in order to survive. Later, believing them to be efficient, I maintained the habit. With time I even reinforced my habit. And then these same palliatives formed ever-increasing layers of protection, so dense that I eventually found myself imprisoned in a terrible impregnable fortress! It was at this point that I had to make the reverse journey in order to rediscover the path through life. Using an unexpected break to my advantage, I started to take down the granite blocks which I had been at such pains to build up. Today, of all that weaponry of palliatives, only tobacco remains. Of which I make very good use.

No civilisation has managed to move on through time without these soothing substances to dull anxiety and delay, if only for a moment, the aggression we feel towards others. Of all those palliatives, tobacco, although addictive, is one of the rare substances which does not alter behaviour. The Amerindians understood this well when they smoked peace pipes, they who were more decimated by the Conquistadors than by their smoking habits.

The State is still trying to make smokers feel guilty with the warnings on cigarette packets. In Brazil, smokers have a choice between two warnings: "Smoking causes cancer" and "Smoking makes you impotent". When they go to buy their cigarettes they say loud and clear : “I want the ones that cause cancer, not the others.” The Canadians shouldn’t be too quick to laugh. Hoping to combat passive smoking, their packets now read : “Smoking may cause fatal diseases in non-smokers”. Finally, that doesn’t seem as stupid as all that. For if non-smokers suffer from fatal diseases, this is in fact what we see every day. Several of my non-smoking friends are dead, having barely reached fifty, after haranguing me ceaselessly until they were simply no longer there to do so. I’d as well tell them that their children had more chance of being run down by a drunk driver than being killed by my cigarette; they would have none of it. This was how, for some years, I returned to Paris every three or four months to be with a friend who was making his final journey. It was even more difficult when his last resting place was replaced by a crematorium where his wife clung lovingly to the urn filled with his ashes which had barely had a chance to cool. I was going to say that even when he was dead he no longer existed. But our good humour returned during the meals which followed those emotional times. Too many pent-up sorrows burst the sluice gate and hearty guffaws of redemptory laughter came over us as we remembered the good times we had shared. This is why I always prefer funerals to weddings. It’s always more difficult to have a hearty laugh with the family-in-law that you don’t really know yet.

Why, then, did all these friends depart so quickly? Didn’t they have good clean lungs without blemish or stain? Yes, but that wasn’t enough. In order to function you need more than perfect lungs if the rest of you is falling apart, eaten away by worry, or if those lungs are simply pulling a body full of drugs and alcohol. Sometimes a shadow on the lungs is less dangerous than shading oneself from the reality of life. Of all the crutches that Man has invented for himself in order to keep going, tobacco is the least dangerous for both himself and others. Without this peace pipe, Man's inherently aggressive nature would turn more quickly to acts of violence. This can be easily observed in the descriptions of criminal characters: "He was a good father, a good husband, a good neighbour, a good employee, he didn't drink, didn't smoke, was always very polite; in fact he had no real faults!" Well yes, he had one very large fault: he had not found any palliatives wherein he might direct his aggressive urges. So, he "blew his top". Take England, where there has been a marked increase in the gratuitous murders of adolescents who have been knifed, since the introduction of the ban on smoking. A world without palliatives would be intolerable. It's better to smoke a cigarette than kill your neighbour. The palliative is life.

"Like many people I have tried to stop smoking. Alas, I even managed it!" a friend told me. Indeed, he hadn't yet found another palliative to replace the old one. All too often, it is alcohol which fulfills this role (as indicated by the increase in alcohol sales in those countries which have embraced the smoking ban); which is hardly going to make things any better. Or, as in the Netherlands, where tobacco, but not cannabis, is now banned in bars. Yet cannabis causes five times the damage to lungs compared to tobacco [10] and increases the risk of schizophrenia by 40% [11]. Even in France, it is interesting to note the coincidence of smoking bans with an increase in movements in favour of the free use of so-called soft drugs, movements often supported by some of our new ministers (Those that The *Guardian* considers to be "neo-crazy").

At that happy time when restaurants still had smoking and non-smoking rooms, a Dublin restaurant owner told me that the non-smoking area tables were filled by 6.30 p.m. and that the smoking area didn't start to fill up until 9.00 p.m. Smokers are often people who take the risk of living. Now restaurants are less happy places. As was confirmed by that famous comedian who did not smoke but who, whenever he took a train, liked to travel in the smoking compartments because he found the passengers were less sad. In my little town the owner of a pub has installed a small, fairly airy room for smokers. This is where the less sad regulars can be found. With the help of some good Irish humour and Guinness, this is where it's at. The non-smokers, drawn by the bursts of laughter, crowd into the back room, thereby forcing the owner to stick a notice on the door: "Non-smokers not allowed".

I remember Professor Schwartzenberg, a renowned cancer specialist, saying that when he was teaching young surgeons how to perform operations on the lungs, they used to go out into the corridor between shifts to smoke a cigarette. Stress has to be fought off with the aid of palliatives. The doctors who smoke the most are those working in Accident & Emergency departments. A cigarette is less dangerous than a glass of whiskey, both for themselves and their subsequent operations.

I can't help but relate a few salient facts regarding our new *ayatollahs*.

Numerous articles have been published to mark the centenary of the birth of Jean Paul Sartre. In all the photographs, our *ayatollahs* have taken great care to erase his legendary *Gitane*.

The same procedure has been followed for a famous singer who died of cirrhosis of the liver. For the tenth anniversary of his death, he appears in the photographs with his glass, but the cigarette has been carefully removed!

Leo Ferré wrote and sang:

"You gave me Paradise
You are my Gitane and that's enough
You are my Gitane, my friend"

This song has been withdrawn from his collected works!

All allusions to tobacco have been withdrawn from Molière!

The British Medical Association is seeking to ban 18 year olds from all films in which someone is seen smoking! Bye-bye *Casablanca* and *Citizen Kane*!

A handcuffed prisoner was seen smoking a cigarette which the two police officers accompanying him had allowed him to light before boarding a train, The *ayatollahs* appeared on the scene to reprimand the officers: "You're there to enforce the law, how can you possibly allow a prisoner to smoke on a station platform!"

On a breezy station platform in Kent, a young man was smoking a cigarette whilst waiting for his train to arrive. An *ayatollah* (*ess*?) arrived on the scene to tell him to stop. The young man waited until the next day to push her onto the railway tracks. Although he was sentenced to prison, a few journalists rose to his defence. May fate be kind to them, all is not lost! [12]

Professor Jérôme Allain, head surgeon at the Henri Mondor hospital on the outskirts of Paris, told me that when he was invited to a conference in Florida, he was smoking a cigarette in front of the building with some fellow surgeons when an *ayatollah* (*ess*?) jogging along the opposite side of the avenue, spotted the smoke rising in circles above their learned heads. She made straight for them and in all seriousness proceeded to reprimand them: "You are killing me!" The eminent professor, whose mind was far from cloudy, came back with the speedy reply: "I'm very happy to hear that."

Jogging is an addictive drug which is as dangerous as any other. As with all drugs, excuses are found: "I'm doing it for my health." Leave well alone that which works well… and so I smile when I see one of them keel over from a heart attack. The worst example of all was when a well-known illustrator who was undergoing endurance tests, that is running on a moving belt, collapsed surrounded by three doctors.

Some British soldiers taken hostage in Iraq were freed in Iran after what one can only imagine to have been a harrowing time. In the photograph showing their liberation, two of them were smoking their first cigarette. The British Minister for Health, Patricia Hewitt, immediately declared: "It is really deplorable that these hostages were shown smoking, it's a bad message for our youth!" Of course the war in Iraq, with the hundreds of thousands of deaths and torture is a much better message for young people.

If the first cigarette of those hostages was criticised, then the last cigarette was refused to someone condemned to death in Florida, under the pretext that death row is a strictly smoke-free zone!

The latest thing from the *ayatollahs*: the poster showing Monsieur Hulot on holiday with his legendary pipe in the Jaques Tati film has just been withdrawn from public display. Likewise, that which shows Coco Chanel with her cigarette! No doubt the *ayatollahs* are annoyed that it took eighty-seven years of cigarettes to finish her off, someone whose style would be the hallmark of the twentieth century even though she didn't even know how to sew!

It is a well-known fact that puritans and self-righteous people have never been associated with creativity. Let us not forget that Senecus gave us Nero and Marcus Aurelius gave us Commodius… which is something to think about!

Yet these new *ayatollahs* have found new battlegrounds: they are now getting worked up about incense sticks in Buddhist temples. A stick of incense is as harmful as a cigarette! So they say. Heavens! Thai monks are in great danger. Close all the temples quickly. It's not dictatorships which are the cause of deaths, but incense…

Since infections picked up during benign operations are dangerous, we'd better close all the hospitals too… They've already started: it's now forbidden to take a cup of tea from the cafeteria to one's room because a child may run past, knock the drink out of your hand and burn himself!

The latest brainwave from the *ayatollahs*: it is now forbidden to throw your mortarboard into the air when receiving your degree as this traditional headgear may come down and injure someone! Students are not allowed to express their pleasure and triumph. Thank you to the killjoys. And don't forget, young people must simply not take any risks. What a lesson for life! Just as in schools you are now not allowed to run in the playground…

Here's yet another discovery those *ayatollahs* have hit upon: plastic baby bottles are now forbidden. There's one other solution: to breastfeed. Alas here we find ourselves confronted by a problem of a moral order: take the young woman who was breastfeeding her baby before a Delta Airlines flight took off. The steward, on seeing her do so, came to tell her that he found it offensive and that he would bring her a blanket to cover herself. When she refused the ground staff who had been contacted regarding the dilemma, asked her to leave the plane [13]. In my establishment breastfeeding is openly encouraged. My guests enjoy their rights to the full.

Rest assured you good people; the *ayatollahs* are here for a good while yet. By not allowing photographs of the cigars and cigarettes of eighty-year old smokers

(Sartre, Freud, Lacan, Roosevelt) they are indulging in a post mortem vengeance. Yet some stubborn examples persist; such as Henry Allingham, founder of the RAF who, on his 112th birthday, announced that the secret of his longevity was cigarettes and women, even though, say some sceptics, at such an age that's the only thing you remember. Or, take that last survivor of the Great War who smoked his pipe until he was 110 years old. Then there are those sporting celebrities who show no intention of stopping [14]. It helps them to relax, they say, in high-pressure competitions. But they shouldn't be mentioned as they are very bad examples for the younger generation.

If your future is bright, safe and secure, you won't feel the need to smoke as much. You might even, at the very worst, be able to stop (I sincerely hope you can. No jokes.) But if the future ahead of you looks dark, and worry creeps over you and money problems grow ever more present, you might find yourself turning to tobacco for a (momentary) respite which, although it is strongly linked to a chemical addiction, answers largely to a psychological need, one of the last little pleasures left to the less well-off classes in our society. This is why the *ayatollahs*' wish to increase the price of tobacco (so that poorer people will spend more of the little money they have on food and less on cigarettes) is such nonsense! It won't discourage those more better-off people in the least, but will certainly be a blow to the poor by increasing their anxiety and, as a logical consequence, their desire to smoke. This process has been studied by Cass Sunstein under the name of liberal paternity. Such a theory would wipe out everybody's bad habits and force them to take up a better life style. An experiment based on this idea was tried out in Scotland where the Tayside Health Authority offered food coupons to those smokers who decided to quit! As this was not aiming at the real problem, failure was inevitable. You can't cure an ill by only looking at the consequences! Poverty can't be wiped out by putting up the price of tobacco! [15]

And cancer, what are you doing about that? I'm looking after it very well thank-you. You can't imagine that, like everyone else, I haven't had my share of traumas, stress, hope and despair. I have so far, more or less consciously, managed to deal with them in such a way that my desire to live is the stronger of all these influences. The alcoholic and smoking abuse that my body has undergone, at times to an excessive degree, have not got the upper hand. Let me try to shed light on this matter by referring to decades of personal experience, decades of psychoanalytic experience and decades of experience in love. Without forgetting those experiences of close, non-smoker friends who have been felled like a line of trees, consumed by the deathly shadows of lung cancer when they had barely reached fifty. It has to be seen that all the research into the causes of cancer has focused on the biological data in the search for a direct explanation, thereby ignoring the complexity of the interaction between psychology and biology. The real issue is not what causes cancer, but *how* is cancer caused. They have never found a vaccine and probably never will, since you would have to find a vaccine against all those deathly forces inherent in all human nature.

The forces of life can be suppressed for many objective or unconscious reasons. For example, the new-born baby who demands his feed "body and soul". He learns to resist the aggression arising from unsatisfied hunger, something which is experienced as a violent reaction and must find an outlet somewhere. This avoidance of aggression is indelibly inscribed in his neurones and, at that age, will precede consciousness. If such aggression continues and is repeated too often, it will eventually get the upper hand (something which

Freud incorrectly called our innate nature) and will eventually weaken or worse, suffocate, the very force of life (mothers of children with cancer should learn to read every expression of irritation which their child is unable to formulate and learn to respond so that the new-born child may place himself in the outside world.) Such experiences of aggression lead to unconscious physical defence mechanisms which themselves express our inability to confront aggression (whether internal or external) and which manifest themselves in the form of a particular tumour or lymphoma within the body.

Those aggressions which irritate the body may be external: physical factors (pollution, tobacco, alcohol, radiation, drugs) or internal: psychological factors (emotional, stress, bereavement.) Those psychological factors are more powerful than the physical ones, for they represent an attack on the very forces of life by negative currents which are all the more powerful for being unconscious. Furthermore, these internal aggressions are much more dangerous, for the chemical reactions produced by the body's defence mechanisms when under attack in a repeated and intensive manner, then attack the neurones. Chronic anxiety leads to the overworking of the adrenal glands. Whereas, faced with external aggressions, our immune system produces antibodies, antigens, white blood cells, benign cysts, against internal aggressions there is no protective screen; they therefore have direct access to the different organs and their cells. These internal aggressions act like the crows in the famous Spanish proverb: *Cria cuevros, te sacaran los ojos* (Rear crows and they will eat out your eyes.) The hydrochloric acid produced by our bodies when we are under stress eats away at the stomach. Internal emotional aggressions which we allow to develop and which at times we more or les consciously sustain, are like the Spanish crows for we ourselves have fed them.

Since my adolescence I have always wanted to try and understand the why of how things are done. The conventional *lycée* education did not, however, suit me. I somehow never managed to arouse enough interest in the subjects we were made to study. At 18 years of age I found myself in an administrative post in a shipping agency in Casablanca. In spite of the shining future which the director foresaw for me, I resigned in order to write "my book". "Mr Chatenoud, I will never read your book," was the reply from the very British director.

I returned to Paris when I was 24 and passed the exams to study a degree in literature, followed by a degree in philosophy at the Sorbonne. Apart from the fact that I formed a friendship with Vladimir Jankélévitch, who later had the kindness to support my book shop, I never managed to bow to the teachings of the university. Wasn't it Kepler who said, in spite of the universities' acknowledgement of his laws in astronomics: "University is the guardian of ignorance." So my unconscious and I undertook to follow several enthralling chunks of pschoanalytic study, first Freudian, then Jungian and finally to Lacan.

I liked Lacan's "style" and admired what he brought to an understanding of Freud. For two years I followed his seminars. His perfectly blue-grey hair and his perfectly crooked Italian cigar were all part of the show. Contrary to most of his listeners, I never took notes. I let the whole experience flow into me. As much his, as that of his auditors. When I saw all those bowed heads busy noting down the merest word of the 'master', it all got on my nerves. Feeling captivated by his discourse, as much as by his mannerisms, my attention was fully taken up and I had no time to take notes. I believe I understood and appreciated him more than many of those scribblers who were hanging on every word. It was only much later that I discovered that Pythagoras forbade his students to take notes. Now I understand why.

It is only now that this continual search has come to mean something of capital importance. By bringing to my consciousness the profound aggression of all the diffuse and confused feelings that my curious nature had imposed on my body, this search played a moderating role in the sense that it acted as a filter to soften and anaesthetize the emotional aggressions which had been so powerful. Now a part of those internal defence mechanisms which had been working overtime, had been taken care of.

During those years of searching, to that unconscious appeaser of internal aggression, I first added alcohol, which for the past fifteen years, I have replaced by cigarettes. These external aggressions which I inflicted on my body, contrary to what one might believe, were not added to the preceding ones, but took care, thanks to the antibodies, of another part of my defence mechanism, thus diminishing the risk of the development of cancerous cells. These defences showed themselves, in my case, in the form of a benign tumour of the parotid gland and another situated in the lymph nodes.

I can therefore say today that thanks to my enquiring spirit which is still alive and well, with the help of cigarettes and alcohol, I have kept those cancerous cells at bay. And I believe I will go on doing so for a long time yet.

Paradoxically, alcohol and tobacco (external factors) can help to suppress emotional aggressions (internal factors). It is much more dangerous to look to external factors (to stop smoking) for the internal factors are always left bare, with no screen, no filter so that the body experiencing these uncontrolled feelings which have been freed in this way, will become the target of cancerous developments.

This explains why some cancers can be seen to develop in people who stopped smoking months ago. How many times have I heard: "It's just too bad, he stopped smoking so many months ago!"

It also explains those heavy smokers who never get cancer, like the Londoner, Beatrice Langley, who lit her cigarette on the flame of the birthday candles which marked her hundredth birthday.

It is why one of my friends, who was a native of a small island off Connemara and who had never smoked nor drunk alcohol, left this life when she was barely twenty-five years old, in spite of her love for her young children. She had been unable to fight off the internal damage that life on the "mainland" had come to signify for her.

Those doctors who are only interested in the biological causes will tell you that it's passive smoking which killed her... Or that it's genetic and hereditary; the proof - people of Asian origin who immigrate to the USA show the same incidence of cancer as the Americans within one generation. Well of course it must be genetic...

It is not surprising that Ireland is one of the countries where the rate of cancer is the highest in Europe. Having suffered centuries of English domination, they have learnt to suffer in silence. One of their favourite expressions when faced with the slightest problem is "Paul, say nothing". Faced with such repression of internal emotional aggression, how could the body react otherwise?

The majority of cancer specialists with whom I have shared my reflections, nod in agreement saying: "We agree with you, but we can't say it." To my knowledge, only doctor Frederick Levenson has committed himself in writing. I would like to thank him for that here. [16]

A period of remission following treatment has often been noted and this can easily be explained by the fact that the symptoms have been dealt with by the external agression which has been endured: surgical intervention, radiotherapy, chemotherapy. These things calm the internal destructive aggressions. But when the effects of the external aggression decrease, the symptoms reappear. Sometimes there are unexpected sudden external aggressions which look after the latent internal aggressions.

I had one such experience about fifteen years ago when, no doubt under the influence of the *ayatollahs*, I had decided to give up smoking. I had been wearing a patch on my arm for a few days when I was seized with an irresistible urge to smoke. After two remedial puffs I fell unconscious to the floor. Some time later I came to, lying on the floor of my cottage. A friend who happened to come by to see me, alerted the emergency services. The nurse who held my hand while I was transferred to hospital, was visibly relieved to have got me to the Accident & Emergency department still alive. The doctors diagnosed a heart attack, explaining that I was not the first to experience such a thing in the circumstances. This diagnosis was later confirmed by the Parisian cardiologists whom I consulted! They underlined the fact that in general, it proved to be fatal. Since that time my steel heart (the cardiologist's very words), although dented, tolerates my use of tobacco.

It is these diverse external aggressions (heart attacks, all manner of benign tumours) that have protected me from the development of a possible cancer, by keeping my body busy trying to fight off the psychosomatic reactions. Some doctors have expressed their disdain, bordering on condescension, with regard to my analysis of cancer. How could they react otherwise? The medical profession, which holds so much power, could hardly tolerate being called into question. Unfortunately for them, numerous readers fully agree with my analysis, citing both personal and family experience.

Once again, dealing with the consequences and not the causes never resolves a problem. Certain people are obsessed with everything that might be carcinogenic, as much in the environment as in food. This obsession can in itself become a source of stress, so much so that the wish to protect oneself at all costs can actually have the reverse effect and create an additional internal aggression.

Take the fact that nowadays the media regularly warns us about everything which might be carcinogenic: sauces, tobacco, saccharine, sun, X rays, microwaves, polluted air, alcohol, red meat, pills, fat, barbecues, vinegar, industrial pollutants, electromagnetic waves, mercury, even vitamins, salt… I am sure that before this book is published our *ayatollahs* will have found others. I consume all of them and am doing very well.

Latest discovery: professor Naomi Allen of Oxford University has just published a study in *The Journal of the National Cancer Institute* which sets out to prove that one glass of wine per day may increase the risk of cancer by 0,7 per thousand!!! And, she says, if alcohol reduces the risk of cancer of the thyroid, it increases the risk of cancer of the anus. "To drink or to have an enema, the choice is yours!" This is the latest slogan from our *ayatollahs*. [17]

It's by looking first to internal aggressions that we may restore calm, as happened to me one evening when I received a couple of friends with their month-old baby. We had put the infant in a room adjoining the dining room. It was his first trip. Feeling lost in this new place he wouldn't stop crying. His mother was at a loss as to how to reassure him. I offered to do so. Entering the room, I spoke to him calmly telling him that his mummy and daddy were there, that they were going to have dinner and everything was fine and he could have a rest. He immediately stopped crying, to the astonishment of his parents who asked me what I could possibly have done to him. "I simply reassured him," I said. Taking care of internal aggression, or, as it happened, anxiety and fear, is more important than all the rest. More, for example, than putting a dummy in his mouth…

So leave me to smoke in peace, and if the *ayatollahs* continue to lecture to us poor unrepentant smokers, we will surely be left with no alternative but to find other ways out by enriching those tour operators who organise smoking week-ends, in smoker airplanes (*Smintair*) and restaurants and bars where smoking is allowed in countries like Austria, Switzerland, Belgium and Estonia where hospitality still means something.

Latest discovery: the researchers Arul Chinnaiyan and Christopher Beecher have just managed to isolate the molecule which accelerates the growth of metastases; it's called sarcosine. So that's what it was. Quick, we must do everything in our power to neutralize this destructive molecule! For a high level of sarcosine is an indicator that the disease is spreading rapidly. [18]

Last latest discovery: at last some good news; fighting HIV with tobacco. Professor Julian Ma and Professor Rainer Fischer (Saint George's, University of London) have discovered that the tobacco plant could be used as a topical microbicide which would neutralize the HIV virus. [19]

That afternoon I walked along the beach once more, quietly, under the rain. I was recovering from the previous evening. I had been to a wake. I was beginning to accustom myself to this ritual which was part of village life. Without knowing the family particularly well, it is considered the duty of every person to pay one last visit to the deceased. In accordance with this tradition I had therefore called on the Gallaghans to pay my last respects to the grandmother who had just passed away at the age of 96.

With her gracious smile, the mistress of the house had just offered me a slice of cake and a cup of tea. It was then that Seamus, standing a few paces away, fell down without a sound, seized by a heart attack, his mouth barely contorted by a slight pain, his eye fixed in a vacant stare. Neither the doctor friend nor the priest (a nephew) had time to act in their capacities. Death, with this second blow, wiped the smiles off the faces of those who had gathered to spend a quiet evening together. Judging my presence to be of little use, I passed in front of a row of stunned faces and made for my car. Peter, who accompanied me as far as the gate, told me with some difficulty that Seamus' father had died in exactly the same way; a heart attack at a wake. The paternal example persists. To the very end. To think that there are still those who confuse their parents' example, which is transmitted from one generation to another, with biological heredity...

Like my forty-year old friend who died the day his son was born, as his father had done when he himself was born, and his grandfather on the day his father was born...

A few years later my oldest sister died in exactly the same circumstances as my father and at the same age: a stroke sustained during a meal.

A fitting revenge for the unconscious, which she so strongly rejected... For my young son's birthday she had given him a toy car:

"I hope you realise that this car is not just any old car," I said to her, "it's the car mother went to hospital in, never to return."

"Oh, you always want to analyse everything. I'll tell you how I bought it: in the toy shop there were hundreds of little cars, and I don't know why I chose that one, but I could just as well have chosen another."

The "I don't know why" which made her choose that model and that colour were unsayable things for the little girl who had never seen her mother again. That which is not said will out, some other way. For fifty years she had been carrying that symbolic car, which finally reappeared in the real form of a smaller version on the occasion of a birthday. (I admire the ingenuity of the unconscious which managed to pick out the exact model, to the very year and colour, of the one thing that had been so denied and so longed for.)

In the deep silence of the night on this peninsula at the extreme edge of Europe I thought about my father. He had been injured on the Chemin des Dames [20] during the Great War. As for myself, I have spent my life travelling along this road and was hurt more than once. After the war he left for Morocco where he spent the rest of his life. As for myself, it was on Irish soil that I threw down my anchor. The similarities are greater than would appear. The same bare hills, the cottages with their thatched roofs which come close to the Moroccan *noualas*, the warm smile and generosity of the inhabitants, the little treeless roads which follow the old tracks, the same paraffin lamps as those I knew in my childhood, the same ocean which covers me in its salty spray. Seeing the fine wands of water thrown up in my rear view mirror, as I drive along, I see the clouds of dust, which as children, we saw from a long way off on the track, and which told us that our father was on his way home, long before we could either see his car or hear its engine. Finally, as guttural as Arabic, Gaelic has many grammatical similarities and words which mean the same thing (like, for instance, "woman"). And on the postcard which depicts my cottage, there appears in the foliage of the tree which hovers above it, an incredibly detailed outline of my mother's image, she who died in Morocco so long ago. Everything is changed and yet everything is there.

When my father died I wrote these verses which I came across:

"My father has died.
The bed canopy is on the roof
And underneath there is you.
A pretty flower in a deserted factory.
A piece of precious wood lying on a building site
The smile of an Algerian
The fatuousness of a man from the North`
The self-assurance of a South-African
In the Revard, the poverty of Félicien,
In the cold, his death near his still
The tears of Martha
His abandoned wife.
The intuition and the unique strength of my vision
In the lucid smile of Emilie."

A few days after his death, I felt the need to go to Morocco and see the place where he had spent his life and where I had been born. I went also to pay my filial respects to those that had known him and to share my grief with them. My first visit was to the person who had shared this Moroccan adventure with him at a time when they were both single young men. The old man greeted me on his doorstep with these words: “You know, young man, I didn’t owe your father any money.”

It took me a few minutes to take this in. When at last I was able to do so, a sardonic laugh allowed me to swallow my request for love. For it was this that I had come looking for; yet the dear fellow could hardly understand that a young man would make such a journey just for “that”. My second visit was to the Morrocan corporal who had shared my father’s fate for several decades. The path leading to his house was drenched; I had to abandon my car and continue on foot in my smart shoes. Several scrawny dogs were circling around the old abode, barking noisily. A hundred-year old woman appeared, bent double by illness and age. She almost straightened up with a start at the apparition before her: a young man in a white shirt and tie heading towards her in the rain, up to his ankles in mud. After having explained who I was, her son came forward, his sixty years of sun and hard work were plainly visible. I gave them the news; the women began to wail. Knowing that this was their custom, I was able to contain my emotion. Whereas, when the eyes of the old man filled with tears, my own fell with his in silence.

While they offered me mint tea, they cleaned my shoes. Then the old man harnessed an old cart to an old horse to take me back to my car. The beast, which looked more like a donkey than a horse, could barely move the cart through the thick mud, while the rain effortlessly combined with the tears on the faces of the old man and the young, in the silence of that greyest of days.

Father’s death played more than one trick on me. In the little smokey pub I didn’t see my female Swedish neighbour’s brown mane of hair tremble as my hostess questioned me about my past life as a book shop owner in Paris (I had opened the first music book shop in Paris).

I have just heard a former French Minister for Defence express his regret that he never ran a book shop and that he had never had a cottage in Ireland. I myself have never regretted not being Minister for Defence.

In every country throughout the world a book shop owner goes around with a little halo over his head which indicates that he is knowledgeable. My colleague, José Corti, whom I visited as often as possible, fed me with his anecdotes. Such as the one about the client who asked him for a book: "It's called 'Camus'*Plague*' but I don't know the name of the author." When commenting to yet another soul, that all this was hardly very Cartesian, back came the reply: "Oh my, who knows Cartes these days!"

I invited him to pay me a visit in my book shop, he told me that since his son had been taken away by the Gestapo never to return, he had not ventured further than the Boulevard Saint-Michel. At this point the telephone rang:

"A book about India ? What is the exact title?"

"Do you at least know the author's name?"

"Ah, it was a lovely book with a beautiful cover that somebody lent you and which you've now mislaid! That's going to be very difficult."

And finally:

"Madame, save your despair for those things that really matter in life."

That was José Corti; a great doyen of letters who was never condescending or disdainful of his customers who were sometimes rather ignorant. His legendary patience proved a good lesson for myself. He had also been the instigator of the *La Pléiade* editions. I couldn't pass over his name without sharing my admiration for him.

I did not escape this myth which attaches itself to book shop owners and which I forced myself to dismantle.

Far from reading all the books which surround him, the book shop owner barely knows the blurb on the back cover. Far from meeting writers, he more often meets authors enquiring as to how their books are selling. He knows the size and shape of the volumes he is handling better than their content and the book shop owner's physical strength is as important as his intellectual aptitude. On his sturdy shelves, stacked side by side, lie ideas which are completely foreign to him. The book shop owner is also the person who gaily ascends the ladder without demeaning himself, while his clients dare not mount higher than the first rung for fear of falling. The bookshop owner is all that and more. He is the lover of books. He is the object of love that the young dark-haired Swedish woman saw in him. It was only later that I learnt that her fluttering eyelids were for her father who had just died and who had also owned a book shop.

Once again the unsayable had woven its web. Thanks to the Guinness, the lost paradise of her father was there, in the familiar guise of an unknown book shop owner. She found me charming. I thought that my charm was at work. She didn't know that at that moment I was nothing but an unknown fantasy, he who gives form to that which cannot be expressed. From whence the strength of the resulting love... Love is specific to the imagination of each individual. The unknown book shop owner had become the object upon which such a love could be bestowed. Her imagination had found a bodily form (mine) and was thus entering the realm of reality.

It was this tangible misunderstanding that I wanted to discern and then pinpoint (I don't know why, but I love *her*). After the event I didn't enjoy the feeling of being "only" the standard bearer of the other person's imagination, whereas I had considered myself the apple of her eye. Dousing oneself in androsterone is not enough for the oxytocin to be aroused with the help of pheromones, which I will leave to biologists, since it so amuses them. This is the point at which the try must be converted into a goal. And that's where everything starts: misunderstanding or sublimation when two unconscious minds meet and it's the right moment... At times this hidden fantasy, this unsayable thing is much more difficult to unravel, existing outside time, it may arise from the depths of childhood and grows not old. The eye of the ventriloquist is without age.

Just as the flowers I came across in a meadow had always been there: it was in February, the fuchsias had started to bud, the daffodils were in bloom and the nearby Gulf Stream had given spring a little jolt. The first wild rosebuds looked down on the snowdrops which were now sadly wilting away. Coming back across the fields from my daily walk, I found myself inside a perfect rectangle of daffodils. All around me, for a good twenty or so metres, they were growing in regular lines for no apparent reason. A few weeks later I met the owner of this field and was given the answer to the enigma: That was my mother who planted them at the beginning of the century because that was where our house was. I knocked it down thirty years ago to build a new one lower down. There was not a single trace of the old house and yet every year the daffodils continued to bloom. This revelation led me to wonder, for I too had planted a few flowers around my cottage, without thinking that they might survive the building.

A few months later, while crossing an old cemetery where a few Celtic crosses, worn by the wind, still poked their heads over the stone wall, I came across the mother's grave, quite by chance. It was in a beautiful setting. With the ocean down below, it seemed to highlight the green meadows dotted with sheep. The fine rain, old crooked tombstones, the Gaelic inscriptions half worn away and a few scattered succulents and I was struck by a curious feeling. The sight of such a landscape made me want to lie down and stay there for ever, my sense of aestheticism having won the day over life itself. I had a notion of going to pick a few of 'her' daffodils and laying them by her side. I never did.

On the other hand, I did speak to the young woman sitting beside me in the aeroplane as I flew back to Dublin one day. The flight was very pleasant, interrupted only by the mumbling announcements from the captain. Every airline company goes to great lengths to make these passenger announcements as incomprehensible as possible.

"Would you like me to translate what the captain is rambling on about?"

"Well, as a matter of fact I didn't really understand," she said politely, not wanting to admit that she hadn't understood a thing.

"He said: Don't think for a minute you're the important people here, the only man in charge is me and I don't give a damn about you."

She burst out laughing and added:

"You know he's made a mistake about me, for my importance is relative, I earn my living as a prostitute."

Surprised, but not thrown off balance, I extricated myself neatly:

"Then he owes you every respect, for your profession is much older than his and you must know a lot more about human relations than he."

We continued to talk. No doubt touched by the fact that my attitude remained unchanged, regardless of her revelation, she thanked me with a friendly smile. This friendship was to last a very long time.

At the time of my stormy youth, when my sexual desires engulfed me unexpectedly, my completely unromantic and unaffectionate desires led me to frequent prostitutes. I thought what I was doing had no implication whatsoever. Nothing could have been further from the truth. An empathy formed in spite of myself. Things came to a head one day when a certain young woman insisted, once our business was over, on inviting me to dinner. I still remember her, even though a lot of other so-called love affairs have drifted away in the mists of time. Which makes me think of that magistrate in Orléans who, finding himself faced with a prostitute upon whom he was obliged to pass judgment, fell in love and decided to marry her. He was struck off the list of magistrates.

Yet the courtesan, Loys, told us long ago: "Moralists knock on my door just as much as anyone else." Or, to put it another way, without quoting eminent men of the cloth, the higher the spiritual quest, the more unavowed and hidden desires will surface. Take Saint Theresa of Avila or that young woman who wanted to escape the suffocating world of the Amish people. Unable to live by her songs alone, she became a prostitute. Then one day, she saw her bearded uncle, the most rigid man within the sect, coming into the club where she worked. My profligate curiosity led me into the world of orgies. It wasn't a world of rampant sexuality that I found however, but one of love and friendship. My companion and I walked around hand in hand among naked bodies, occupying themselves on mattresses scattered about. Her husband, well-used to this practice, was a very jealous man. This was therefore the only place we could see each other in peace! (Aristippus, caught going into the house of a courtesan, replied: "it is not going in, but never coming out that would be a real vice.")

You can meet someone anywhere, like that pharmacist who, from behind her counter, saw a man passing in the street. She said to herself "This is the one." It took her several months to track him down. He was married. She managed to get him to divorce and then marry her, she later told me. They have spent forty happy years together. Love is a projection reactivated by a certain silhouette.

We've all had plenty of strange encounters. Here is one among many.

The glow of London's neon lights cast a shadowy pall over the void. I was dining alone in a restaurant. At a neighbouring table, there were three men and a woman, who was facing me. She was smiling and throwing meaningful glances in my direction. As for myself, immersed in my newspaper, I played the blasé intellectual. Wanting to reply to her questioning eyes, I asked for the bill and went out. From a nearby phone box I called the restaurant.

"I would like to speak to the woman sitting with the three men at the table at the back."

A man's voice replied. I hung up then rang again, repeating that I wanted to speak only to the woman. She came to the phone.

"I suppose you know who I am."

"Who you are, no, but where you were five minutes ago, yes."

"When can I see you?"

"Tomorrow morning, at my hotel. Around ten." And she gave me the address.

Twenty years later, our paths crossed again by chance. She reminded me that in the course of our walks around London, I had given her a record of Gustav Mahler.

"Did you know that that record which I often listened to, was what started my daughter off on her musical career?"

Then she told me about her husband and children.

"I have raised my children thinking of you and the values that you embody and which I would like to pass on to them."

Touched and flattered at having become the unknown spiritual father, I sometimes thought of all these children who were on the receiving end of principles from an unknown source, and about how difficult it would be for them to unearth their origins. As for their actual father, a real 'father Joseph' in reverse, he must have had no idea that when he played with his own flesh and blood on his knees, he had been stripped of the fatherly role, since the actual points of reference were elsewhere. If certain men doubt their biological paternity, often quite rightly, those who are delighted to see themselves in the physical resemblance with their children, should not leap up and down in the air too soon. These insidious father Josephs don't realise that those children who look so like them, are in fact born of an unknown spiritual father.

One gesture, one word, can register in a profound way with a child one does not know. An apparently banal gesture, which is often forgotten, might follow him with unsuspected doggedness.

It was in this way that the actor Alain Cuny tells how, as the child of an adulterous union, his uncle, who was a priest, offered family masses, so that God might call in the proof of his mother's sins as quickly as possible. Then one Sunday, alone in his boarding school, a nun took an interest in a small toy which he had made for himself. It was that small gesture on her part which saved my life. Amongst those gestures which kill or save, it sometimes takes very little to change the fate of one individual. Sometimes it hangs by such a slight thread that it barely seems to hang together at all. The path through life is never simple. It's simply our own, that's all. Alain Cuny was a great actor whom I liked very much. He made his first film when he was over eighty years of age. Then he died a few months later, having left both French and Italian cinema the richer for over half a century. He was there for my twentieth in Fellini's *Dolce Vita.* I ran to see every new film this director made and stayed under its spell for a long time afterwards (I can still see today the sea of silver paper in *la nave va*). Then he threw himself into his *Casanova* which I never wanted to see. I have always refused to go and see a film, even a Fellini, which is based on a literary work which I have enjoyed. I can share many things except my imagination. I like to be faced with other people's imagination, but not the one I've already got on board.

Opera is the same. I think that filming an opera is a nonsense. The imagination that the voice works its way into has nothing to do with the physical appearance of the singer. The concert hall in which the performance takes place is also a part of it all. As for the vocal technical perfection which these fairly showy productions are looking for by engaging celebrities, it is for me secondary. There is this other thing which is essential: the voice. The one that rises from the depths in order to speak to us of love. One voice may hide another. The colour and timbre of the voice which moves you the most, are not the result of technical perfection, but something which they evoke in you as an individual.

That unspeakable element in me is aroused more by Pilar Lorengar or Dora Gatta than by La Callas. If there are some musical experts whose unspoken core is more moved by La Callas, then I'm very happy for them. Only they shouldn't impose it on me. My own cannot be aroused by just anyone.

It can sometimes be glimpsed in my ventriloquist's eye. That look which is always on the lookout for the person to whom I could say at a bend in the road: "It is a long time I have never met you." To the one whose imperfections are lost in a happy face, which is my definition of beauty, or the one who is faithful, powerfully, totally, completely, to the slightest aspect of her face and body. My unspoken core and me, we sail straight on, happy to avoid the rocks where the sirens dance. There's no point covering my ears, because with the unspoken you can neither deceive nor be deceived. It's impossible to cheat it. Impossible to betray it either. That's why, when you find it, it is wonderfully too late.

"Too late to make your own mask.
You must drink of that vessel
Or of the *krater* whose handles
Dance for you."

That *crater* was the one in Cornwall. It was one summer's evening. The mist from the ocean had hidden the night which was drawing in. I was coming home from the beach across the fields with a young English woman, when the moon lit up a crater of about thirty metres in diameter.

- It was perhaps made by a meteorite, she said.
- Or by an aeroplane which came down, I said innocently.

This strange site attracted us. Our youth was then drawn into it. Later she told me how her father, who was a fighter pilot, had been mistakenly shot down by the RAF. She was three years old. In her expression, she revealed something that I knew well. Yet I had never told her that my mother had died in similar circumstances when a fighter pilot had crashed not far from her. I wasn't three years old. There are looks which throw the unspoken into your face. You are tarnished by them, and like a poison, they eat away at your insides. My insides were well-used to that particular poison.

One summer's evening, on the west coast of Cornwall, two ventriloquists "believed" they loved each other in the shadow of a *crater*. We shared our planes at our unspoken core. Without even uttering a word, those unspoken things find each other. The unspoken core is that indelible paradise written in the child's heart. That lost paradise sometimes gives way to something intolerable.

This is how Marthe Bibesco recounts her first meeting with Marcel Proust: "*But how could he understand why I wanted to distance myself from him as much as I could? It was because he awoke that fear in me, the fear of that which cannot be spoken.*"

The unspoken core is that which is irretrievably lost and indelibly written. Some would call it "the irresistible attraction", others the *je ne sais quoi* which fascinates us, others again that "indefinable charm". Maupassant called it "that unaccountable seduction" [21]. Maupassant's stories illustrate Freud's theories. In Paris they both followed the teachings of Charcot who replied, to those who denied the existence of the subconscious: "That doesn't stop it from existing."

I used this unspoken core to arouse that of women. It was child's play. Evoke it and content oneself with its reflection and you have Casanova. To persist in the illusory conquest over and over again, is Don Juan. Don't worry, I'm not going to list the derisory catalogue of my conquests, nor of my demises, which would be a lot more instructive. No, I am simply going to illuminate a few small episodes from the lives of those who chose to confide in me:

There was the one who, when very young, obliged her parents to move because she bore too worryingly close a resemblance to the neighbour on the same landing. There could be no doubt as to her real father. She never felt the wish to track him down, she told me (which makes me think of the story of the husband who was such a cuckold that he had to dress up as a neighbour in order to enter his home. I'll tell you about that later.)

There was the one who, on Sunday afternoons, went out and walked up the Champs-Elysées, showing her superbly quivering legs from beneath a mini skirt, just in order to feel the admiring glances bestowed upon her from the men she passed. Then she went back home.

The one who drew her psychological gleanings from her psychiatrist husband who worked in the law courts. Not feeling very charitable, I replied that I didn't doubt his jurisdictional capacities.

The one who hated her father with a vengeance, because when she was young, her mother said to her: "Go and take my place in your father's bed and give him a cuddle." She never thought that the word replace, she told me, would prove so onerous for a little girl. And did she think about the place that the great *cailín* would occupy in this story?

The one who, as the daughter of a well-known and respected company director, was obliged to contend with the presence of her naked father every time she washed herself and then had to suffer his perverse aggression. She never denounced him. I'm not surprised that some people don't like washing.

The one who wrote to me: "I would like to help you build the pedestal that you deserve." A friend who was not very poetic, suggested I send the following telegram: "Send a hundred thousand dollars and I'll build the pedestal…"

The one who was a fake blonde, as she herself would say, only she wouldn't have it said because, after ten years of marriage, her husband still didn't know. "If he knew he would divorce me straight away," she confessed one evening.

The one who deceived her husband by sleeping with his arch enemy and boasted about it. To side with the enemy is to betray oneself. To hate someone to this point is to still depend on them.

The one who never told her children that she had been married before meeting their father. They learnt the truth at the solicitor's office, after the burial. They still haven't got over it.

The one who told me later that she had systematically gone back to all the places I took her to with another man, so that they would not remain linked in her mind solely to myself. If my ego suffered something of a bash, I admired her remedial cure for such amorous nostalgia.

The one whose husband chased me across Paris in order to slay me.

The ones who, more than happy to escape my list, gambol in the meadows, like the Berbers of Tessaoud, with their games and their smiles as their only defence.

It is the privilege of the eye of the ventriloquist to have access to previously unheard confessions (or so they said), even though they declared “this is the first time I’ve deceived my husband”, this privilege was always tinted with scepticism. On the other hand, I understood why some women harboured an indelible hatred or fear of men. That fear so often expressed in the choice of an insignificant husband, or the bearer of purely social importance, which amounts to much the same thing, be he “director” of anything whatsoever. In order to avenge themselves for having been thrashed or humiliated while still young, they finally were the ones who wore the trousers.

To humiliate a child is to mark him forever. Adolf Hitler, Joseph Stalin, Mao Tse-tung and Saddam Hussein among so many others, know something of this. Whatever the political guise used to cover up this childhood humiliation, military riding breeches often clothe a nation’s lost father. This pitiful, gaudy attire is the sign of inextinguishable vengeance.

I do not refer here to the riding breeches of the Maréchal Lyautey of whom Clémenceau said: “Here is a man who has balls on his arse! A pity they are not his own!”

If you did not have a father who humiliated you, you can still become head of state. A father who died before you were born is even better; from Mohammed to Clinton they are legion. All you need is an absent or insignificant father and you can become one of those jokers who are flourishing all over the planet at the moment. It's very easy. With the help of a friend's television channel, or even better, your own, you can rattle off your promises and send the gob-all masses to sleep, which is all they're really asking for. Even the most sinister decisions won't prevent those jokers from being re-elected. It's what is now called getting away with murder, whether it is in Washington, London or Rome. Things are no better in Paris. Because he has a 'Josephine', our Joker seated on his Camargue horse, thinks he's the victor of Eylau. In fact, the only merit he's achieved, is to gloss the grasping pages of 'Hello' with his vulgarity. Before he was elected, a number of the journalists who have stayed here were concerned that the French might elect such a Joker. I reassured them, saying that the French were not that stupid and would never believe the twaddle he was coming out with… I was mistaken. I had simply forgotten that a French doctor, who thirty years ago was thought of as one third worldist and two thirds socialite, was the most publicly adored figure, and that the singer who has sold the most records in my country, was a sad character, so far to the right of the right, that even Eddie Barclay refused to be his producer.

In my defence, our national Joker has been a well-known figure since antiquity. Marcus Aurelius warned me on the subject of this type of elector and his own electorate: "What's so strange about an ignoramus behaving ignorantly?" As for the Joker himself, he had seen him all too clearly: "How vulgar they are, those little politicians who think they're philosophers! The little jerks! If you are called upon to take action, then don't go around telling everyone." Marcus Aurelius didn't need television in order to know whom he was dealing with.

Our Joker had no idea that when you want to be everywhere, you are nowhere.

There's someone else who knew his sort very well; Epictetus, who took the trouble of devoting several paragraphs to him: "You need to be firm, they say. But those decisions must be viable. If you go about things with fanatical energy and even pride yourself on it, I say to you: Man, go seek someone to care for you. But if this inclination really takes hold of you, the damage is beyond hope and can never be righted." Again: "The law should not be something which is dependent on the whims of an idiot. Its discourse guides us toward the correct way to deal with idiots." It seems that he knew the sort very well, for he continues: "Your main concern is knowing how to live in marble-lined apartments, how to be served by slaves, how to have a mob following you, dark-skinned cithara players, tragi-(comic?) actors. As long as you live for these external values, you will gain them more than anyone else, but your principal faculty will be as you desire it: crude and slovenly." He concludes with these words: "As for responsibilities and honours, go and look for children. It is they who are afraid of masks, whereas I know they are but of clay and that there is nothing behind them." Epictetus, the emancipated slave, knew even more on the subject than his master! Diogenes himself said to the Joker: "Don't try to govern before learning to think." But he would have none of it.

Heraclitus himself, only got a glimpse of our Joker, but he is hardly less peremptory: "Presumption sends progress in the opposite direction." The same Heraclitus also rubbed shoulders with the bankers which hover around our Joker: "May Pluto not abandon you, leaving the poverty of your spirit to bear the full light of day." Too late.

Stobaeus too had heard about all this twenty-five centuries ago: "You speak in fine words, but you act very badly." Among his numerous advisors, he could at least have found one, who, to make up for his own lack of culture, could warn him with regard to Hippocrates' words in his situation: "To promote oneself and to be lavish will only arouse disdain." [22] Even some of his electorate were astonished that the Joker wanted to place France under the umbrella of NATO. They had forgotten that both before and after being elected, he was wearing a T-shirt boasting his association with the American Secret Services.[23]

How can you vote for a Joker who claims to be the agent of a foreign power? Our little Joker supposedly even gave the Russian President a fright: "They're still laughing about it in the chanceries," I was told by several ambassadors whom I have received here. There is someone who immediately understood that he was dealing with a Joker and that is the new black President of the United States. There is someone else who still hasn't understood: a former socialist Prime Minister who was said to be chuffed to get a phone call from the Joker: "It's an honour and a rare thing," the man declared quite calmly! "I have changed" the Joker claimed in a sugary voice during an electoral meeting. "The snake too changes his skin, but he is no less a snake for it!" - so goes an African proverb. [24]

Our Joker, who stands on tiptoe for the photo shot, reminds me of another such person. He too was a former Prime Minister. His hair had died, of laughing, for he was too funny. At least he didn't suffer from that ridiculous misfortune of being bald with hair! So his hair had deserted him before his voters. Well-endowed with scandals of one sort or another, he must have said to himself: "Given the law of he who has the most scandal attached, I have every chance of making a comeback." So he made it known that he was ready to serve France again. Our politicians have an annoying tendency to confuse the verb 'to serve' with its opposite when it constitutes the pronominal verb (to help yourself). In fact, he had every chance. Wasn't he the best?

It's not just ministers who conduct themselves in such a cavalier fashion in our good old Republic. Witness this anecdote: Her Majesty the Queen of England, on an official visit to France, found herself on the banks of the Loire. The wife of a minister, wanting to free herself for a moment, entrusted her pink handbag to a high-ranking civil servant who was in their party. Then, considering the item no longer necessary, she left him to look after it for the rest of the ceremony. The poor man had to brandish the poor taste of the Republic for a full two hours. "He had some difficulty keeping his composure in a situation where protocol obliged him to do so," a member of the royal entourage confided in me. I have no reason to doubt the truth of his outrage. True blood never lies!

As for the Italians who have elected their Joker for the third time, they deserve it. Was it not they who invented that wonderful proverb: *La madre degli stupidi é sempre incinta* (The mother of idiots is always pregnant.) the Americans have a saying for those mugs that re-elect their Joker, which is not bad either: The turkeys voted for Thanksgiving.

Montaigne sometimes said that he was tossed from left to right by the press (*presse* meant 'populace' in old French.) In modern French, the suckers are still being tossed from side to side by the press, only they don't know it. Only the Brazilians were quick to realize what was going on: having elected their fancy-looking, television channel-owner, Collor de Mello, with a strong majority, he was forced to resign just two years after he came to power, surrounded by a sizeable crowd, dressed entirely in black. He had asked his followers to come dressed in white, to show their support… the seducer often wins the first round, but rarely the second. Just as in politics, reality cannot be seduced. It creates an illusion for a while and then gives way to disappointment. To see somebody's fragility or intemperance has nothing to do with seduction. At times I am taken for a seducer. They are mistaken; it is only the eye of the ventriloquist that they see. That look that I sometimes shared with those who saw my crutches and my faded crown of the child-king. I was pursued by that sentence, even to the antipodes: "Don't I know you?" The eye of the ventriloquist knows no frontiers, oceans, cultures.

It was when I was coming home one evening to my cottage that I received news of the death of a friend in Paris. I was climbing up the small lane when I saw the faint glow of a lamp that I had left lighted. The gentle flickering of the flame was just visible through the dusty panes of the little window. For a few moments I thought I was entering an unreal world, until the scent of burning turf, drifting across on an invisible strand of smoke, opened my eyes. I rekindled the fire in the wide hearth and grilled a slice of salmon that my friend Paddy had brought me. I opened a bottle of Guinness and poured myself a glass of whiskey. This is how old folk drink here: a slug of whiskey after each draught of Guinness. And that evening I felt old. I thought I had weathered enough not to allow myself to be swept up by emotion. And yet it was there. So I tried to drown my sorrows in drink, but all to no avail as the feelings continued to spill forth. Emotion is the flower of friendship. It's the small flower which takes root in the dirt stuck to the soles of our childhood. It is this flower that we try to brush aside as though it were some childish thing, but which, in the same way that a seed, grows through the rock, forces our outer shell asunder with emotion. It is that little flower which shoots up again, like a lost paradise, like the unspoken core, prompted by unforeseeable events. So, we must not turn aside from this little flower, but rather accept it and allow our tears to moisten it. It is then that life will blossom anew and perhaps, I will become an adult.

Adulthood means becoming free as we affirm the strength of our vision. My own vision is of dreams made real. It is these dreams which have shaped me as I have learnt to cope with financial, emotional or psychological troughs. None of them are insurmountable. As the Irish say: “It’s by going more slowly that you arrive more quickly at your goal.” Along the way I had to brush aside that which was independent of my will, steer round obstacles without letting go of the helm, which simply means steering a course through life right to the very end. At times I had to make myself a pair of wings to fly over the pitfalls. I still use them sometimes, when life decides to throw in my path those unforeseen obstacles inherent in all human existence.

Sometimes I didn’t have time to unfurl them, like the day when I went to the small church at Keraghen to attend the marriage of the youngest in the family. The nave was almost full. One after another, the pink or purple hats, which long gloved hands prevented from flying off, were crowding willy-nilly under the grey church porch, which was far too small to hold so many multicoloured dresses, buttonhole carnations and gleaming shoes. The gusts of rain spared no-one, but the general good humour distracted everyone from these small problems. The escaped strands of hair blown across the girls’ faces just made them all the more lovely. The mother of the groom had her heart in her mouth. In spite of the immense size of her hat, there was an almost animal-like concern in her eyes. In order to quell her anxiety, she grasped my arm and marched me down to the first row of seats. Feeling enthroned at her side, I was moved by such an honour, even though I felt a little awkward at this privilege which was hardly justified. I eventually understood that I was the only person in the assembly who might serve as a barrier between herself and her son, seated in the middle of the chancel. It was thanks to me, at least this is how I like to see it, that Mama's great heart was able to contain itself. After the usual festivities, after the last dance, the newly-weds were about to slip away, when the mother, in a trance-like state, threw herself upon her son. One after another, close friends and associates tried to separate them. The commotion lasted a while for it was more a question of ritual or a game which I had been taken in by. Thinking the bride to be ill at ease, I approached her with a few reassuring words and friendly gestures. She replied in a very relaxed manner, smiling broadly with the unspoken words:

> "My dear fellow, you've been had yet again
> Soon it is I who will be the mother
> And this is no myth."

The bride's lucidity cheered me up. The ridiculous nature of the mother's ritualistic behaviour had worried me. I, the king of mockery, had been caught out. I didn't even have time to spread my emergency wings. It was, of course, that the ritual of this carnal separation beneath the chandeliers of the grand hotel, had reminded me of another one. That which, for so long, had been resonating through the head of the little boy, bent over the edge of a *crater* in the ground, unable to understand how such a small plane could have made such a big hole. Yet I thought I knew how to handle the art of derision successfully when, as a child, I built myself a hut with pieces of metal from the plane that my father had piled up behind the shed. I couldn't understand why he didn't want me to play "over there". "You could hurt yourself," he would say to me. As though I hadn't already been hurt.

And it was there, under the shelter of this debris that I immunised myself. It was there that I imagined I controlled the world, the one that began a long way off, in the very far distance, behind the vastness of this parched terrain, where the sun, worn out as it burned its trajectory across the sky, would set, carrying with it the bloodied dreams of a lost child.

I am still very well immunised: I've never been afraid of flying. The grim reaper tried hard, several times, to ruffle me during flights where the plane was shaken by storms. I refused his entreaties each time. I passed through the turbulence without batting an eyelid.

On the other hand I remember that October evening when my father led me to the orphanage. I can still see his right leg resting on the running board of his car in front of the building. Inside, I clearly remember the little five year-old boy who was in my class at the orphanage. I haven't forgotten his first name in spite of the passing years: he was called David and he was American. I didn't like him.

In my young, blonde head, it was he who had brought the broken wings of the little plane. As for me, I still didn't know how to overcome this obstacle. The unspoken core was buried deep inside me, and the only way it could express itself was by fixing him with my "ventriloquist's eye".

A little later, when I was about ten years old, I would swerve around the overloaded trucks or unpredictable movements of heavily-laden donkeys on my bicycle, as I made my way to school through the thronging streets of Casablanca. My rubber crepe sole would wear through on the front wheel, as I used it to slow the bicycle down. Sometimes, especially on rainy days, I envied my young friends who were driven to school, every morning and evening, by their mothers. Then, one day, it was one of them who, from his wheelchair, envied my bicycle. Crossing the road in order to reach his mother's car, a lorry had run over him. Envy is a terrible fault.

One Sunday evening when I was 14 years old, I took the bus to Rabat, accompanied only by my suitcase which contained all I needed for boarding school. When I arrived the headmaster asked me where my parents were. "I came alone," I replied (and for some weeks I was known as "the one who came alone".) Then he assigned someone to take me to the dormitory and show me my bed. When we reached the foot of the staircase, I was seized by an overwhelming sense of déjà-vu. "Don't bother to come up," I said to him, "I know where my bed is. It's the last but one on the right at the end of the dormitory." I was not wrong. I had never been to Rabat, or to the school. Freud's work had already begun.

As these childhood memories rose from within me in the calm of the night, now well advanced, I went out onto my doorstep. Not a breath of wind. I walked forward onto the lawn and admired the sparkling Milky Way. The beauty of the moment, the beauty of this place, the beauty of the skies and their sidereal iciness held me spellbound. The diffused glow of the stars, barely dimmed by the waning moon, was reflected in the gentle lapping of the ocean, lying stretched out below me. Although I had known the beauty of warm, African nights, I had never really felt the full force of the expression "to take one's breath away". Here, in Ireland, there was one other small element which allowed this expression to assume its full force: impossible to draw breath. More than once, rounding a corner, I had found myself unable to move faced with the simple beauty of the countryside, as I took in this reality for a few moments.

This beautiful, frozen night aroused the memory of various Irish tales, such as this one: On the 1st of May, young virgins are said to go naked to the meadows in order to gather dew before the sun rises. I allowed my imagination to linger on this fantasy, seeing the beautiful young girls, naked as the bog under a full moon. So beautiful they'd take your breath away. Beautiful and naked, like a fairy tale which leaves you completely disarmed. These lovely creatures of the night roaming about the meadows left me feeling limp, and finally, standing speechless beneath the stars, the chill of the night prompted me to go inside.

It was in the warmth of my room, in fact, that another memory resurfaced. Solitude allows random ideas to bounce off one another. After larking around all afternoon, we were walking along one of the quays on the Ile Saint-Louis. The white flanks of the back of Notre-Dame were reflected in the reddening Seine. They say that life hangs but by a thread. Love too. That thread which, before returning to her husband, she removed from my jacket collar. It is because of that hair, that small gesture, my eyes which clouded over with tears, that I remember her, in spite of the passing years. In that one hair I had glimpsed a lost paradise or kingdom. Today I amuse myself by parodying Shakespeare "A hair for my kingdom," but at the time I was quite disarmed. Derision had not yet sounded the alarm.

This was not the only occasion when neither derision nor irony had time to put in an appearance. As a young man, I had gone to a Parisian hospital to seek advice concerning an embarrassing spot. In order to determine the problem more easily, they installed me in a sort of double-door cubicle, where I waited, stripped from the waist down. In this uncomfortable and strange space I waited for the doctor to release me. Half an hour later, a demiurge, no doubt, opened the other door of the cubicle. Like a wolf which had been confined for too long, I shot out of my hole. It was too late to go back: I found myself in an amphitheatre, bursting at the seams with three hundred students, male or female, who were listening to an old bearded professor surrounded by heads of department and their subordinates, as he continued to comment on the preceding case for a further ten minutes.

When he at last turned his attention to me, standing as I was, naked from the waist in front of this terrifying hundred-headed Argus of a medical beast, I was able to mumble a few words about what had brought me there. From his high seat the professor started off again on a rambling discourse on the subject of spots, to finally declare in a theatrical tone: "Now, let us examine the thing." No doubt Brassens had not thought of this, when he declared that he would show his procreative organs to no-one except women and doctors. What to do when they form a common multitude? Alone and still undressed, I did not ask myself what the budding young women doctors might have seen from the heights of their seats of my problem, bared and ripe for examination.

- It's nothing, affirmed the man with the goatee beard in a learned tone
- It's just a sun spot.

Then he bade me return to my cubicle and put my shirt back on. It was then that I felt like spraying the walls of that box with my urine. However, no doubt relieved by the diagnosis, and not wishing to mark my territory in such an inhospitable place, I didn't do it.

I experienced one other hospital misadventure, this time in Ireland. I had gone to a small regional hospital for a benign operation to have a badly-placed screw in my leg removed. I was already naked on the operating table when the anaesthetist, who was a young intern, had asked several rather stupid questions only to then enquire of the surgeon as to how much medication was required in her syringe. Feeling hardly reassured by her lack of experience, I decided to get up and, completely naked, left the operating theatre. I've heard that this event is still talked about on the wards.

It is true that in the course of their lengthy medical studies, students are given no notion of psychology. When we know that 50% of the cure is psychological, it is not hard to understand the difficult position of those who "know". Some people have grasped what is really important in medicine, that it's not the doctor or his medication but the doctor's bag: the sight of him arriving with his bag is half the work done. An empty bag would do the trick. That's not to mention the customary concern normally accorded to the suffering patient. Which reminds me of that pretentious fellow who, not content with ignoring my greeting, cut me off in mid speech when I tried to tell him what had brought me to consult him. "It's me who asks the questions here," he said.

On another occasion I asked for advice from a doctor friend about a growing lump in my parotid gland. "Don't worry, he said, it isn't malignant. I'll give you the address of a friend who will help you." When I called the number, back came the reply to my enquiry "Doctor Durand, the cancer specialist? I'm afraid he has died."

When I did find a qualified and living professor, before operating on me, he asked what my occupation was :

- What does it matter ? I asked.
- The time it takes to heal from an operation can be a simple affair or it can take twice as long. A civil servant who has a regular salary each month will take his time. Whereas the bookseller, as I then was, would have to get on his feet a lot more quickly to look after his shop.

This was exactly what happened. The surgeon's remark was the fruit of his observation and nothing to do with reassuring psycho-speak. It took him 48 hours to inform me of the negative results of the biopsy which arrived at his office. I experienced the same misadventure a few years later. This time over a tumour in my neck glands. I thought that my fate was sealed. I allowed myself to be taken over by the illusion of fear, whereas life continued to speak to me and refused once again to send me the Grim Reaper.

These various experiences helped me to keep death at bay, at least up till now. I don't feel old, even though I have passed the age at which Montaigne thought of himself as follows: "Now I am fifty-five and very old." Sometimes death preys on the very young. Like the adolescent who, undergoing chemotherapy, had to go to school with a shaven head. Out of solidarity, all his friends shaved their heads. Answering a friend's question as to what had become of the young fellow, I could not refrain from throwing her an equally stupid answer: "They all died." Faced with her incredulity, I was obliged to add "without even having time to receive any farewell visits." At times black humour is a foreign territory. Or a foreign language. Don't count on me to translate it.

There's one person who adores posthumous visits. She's a very attractive blonde woman who appears on television every day. She's the prettiest and most well-known of all Irish women. On every news broadcast we see her climb out of a car and go into a house guarded by the police. Her name is Dr Mary Cassidy, state pathologist, turning up at every crime in order to carry out her post mortem examination. Here's a warning to all those budding starlets: fame may come in the form of naked bodies.

That evening I was going to have dinner with friends in a restaurant which overlooks the bay, next to a little port. The fishing boats were barely visible under the rings of circling seagulls. The setting sun caused pink clouds to float above the swell. In the low-ceilinged room, near the window, an eighty-year old couple were breaking open a bottle of champagne with evident joy. Leaving my friends for a few moments, I caught hold of a chair and went, without ceremony, to sit at their table.

You seem in excellent spirits over here… I said by way of introduction.

- Today, she replied, we are celebrating our golden wedding anniversary and, thanks be to God, as you can see, we're very happy. Would you like a glass of champagne?
- Gladly. But what I would really like to know is what is the secret of your fifty years of happiness?
- Oh that's very simple, she said in a loud clear voice to all my friends, who by now were all gathered around the table, my husband always did exactly what he wanted.

Then she whispered in my ear :

- That is to say, everything I wanted!

The only person to share this last remark, I looked at her and smiled. Without breaking our gaze, we raised our glasses in complicity. Then she turned to her husband, I towards my friends, and we all raised our glasses together.

I often thought back to the confiding remark of this octogenerian ventriloquist, whose expression showed the strength and the vision of the kind of assertion which you know inside you to be true. Life's experience had confirmed her intelligence. She had understood that the struggle, be it revolutionary, political or feminist, does not mean taking power in order to do the same thing, as is so often the case, but to take a hand in events so that the order itself is changed. For her the attributes of power are not a goal in themselves. On the contrary, she would say to her husband: "It is I who give you your power." By which we understand: "The power which you use lies with me." It's not a matter of taking the place of a man, but of giving him a place which fulfills him, without feeling he's been taken in.

We find the same satisfaction when men say, by way of deferral before taking a decision, "I'll have to speak to my wife about it." Out of politeness, they say, but in fact they know very well it is she who will decide. At which moment the great *cailín* resumes all her rights, whilst giving him the impression, both with finesse and finally, that it is he who is the boss.

From my cottage on the hill, I can hear, coming from the bottom of the valley, the cries of those feminists:

- And her desires, her pleasure, her independence, you can't just ignore those things?
- Her fulfillment is in being the only one, that unique, irreplaceable person who, fifty years later, is still there as herself to break open the champagne with him. It is to be the one he loves.
- It is what I want most because he has singled me out as unique and for that I am ready to do anything, to be his thing, his object and even, if you don't mind, the object of his pleasure.

The more she understands she is *the* only one, the more she will be able to give herself to being the object of his pleasure. The more she will see herself as "his thing", in the name of love, of course, the more she will feel that what she can give him is irreplaceable. When a man is fulfilled in this way he will feel relieved of the pangs of anxiety. But in order to achieve this, she will have to be even more artful, and have him believe that it is he who desires her, just as she would have him believe that it is he who is the boss. Feeling that this desire is his own, he needs to feel that it is independent, and yet his sexual urges are simply responding to a tender. But this is not what he wants to hear. In order to prove to himself that his desire is autonomous, he will look elsewhere. In this way he can convince himself, at no great expense, that his desire exists outside of her. Yet the whole performance is illusory, and leaves a bitter taste, for the shadow of the great *cailín* is always hovering behind the prostitute or the bombshell who has everything. Penelope's shadow, never fixed and difficult to discern, might at times become blurred, only to be reborn, intangible, indelible, even more powerful through being absent, to bear down with all her weight.

As an eighty-year old, he was not fooled by the role which she had laid out for him over fifty years. He was even rather pleased, as his role simply confirmed his virility. "It is *she* who arouses my desire", he will say to himself, feeling reassured. So, I respond. Forgetting that if *she* did not do this, it would be a complete fiasco.

Sail past the goddesses on the port side, and the sirens on the starboard side, neither your fire nor your song will prevent the ship from sailing on towards Ithaca. Penelope's faith will never be spoken, but symbolised by this thread, woven and unwoven, never denying her femininity or her desire, since Ulysses, as he plays the entertainer on the other side of the ocean, will never fail to cling to it, without ever cutting himself off. Our eighty-year old couple were well entwined. If it was she who drew the threads, he was no more fool in the story as such.

I later found these verses from ancient Egypt…
"My heart is devoted to you,
For you I will do as he bades,
When I lie sleeping in your arms
The desire to respond thus, is the light of my eyes."

(*Beginning of the Songs of Joy*)

Or here:

" She turns his head,
And does as he bades."

(*The Orchard Song*)

Which was not the case of Fiona and Frank, an old Irish couple who spent all their time bickering. After a few insults, Frank would sip his whiskey in the armchair which had been passed down from his grandfather. From the other side of the photograph of the Pope and the Virgin of Lourdes, Fiona would drink her tea. In front of the fireplace where a turf fire smouldered, the dog Jacky and the cat Spicy were dozing, snuggled up together.

- Look, she said, even the dog and cat manage to get on and have a cuddle and we just argue all the time!
- Yes, he replied, but tie them together and you'll see what happens.

Montaigne claimed that "A good marriage, if there is such a thing, refuses both the companionship and conditions of love." To this end, there are mistresses. "Few have married their mistresses without regretting it." [25] But he goes on to confess: "I like to sleep alone, that is to say without a woman, like a king." [26]

Socrates was more doubtful. Asked by a young man whether or not he should take a wife, he replied: "Whatever you do, you will regret it." [27] He was well placed to say so: his wife Xanthippes, in a fit of hysteria, tore up all his clothes. Without losing his composure, he made for the senate dressed only in a blanket which he had seized as his only garment and made his speech paying no heed to the jeering from the assembly.

The almost ninety-year-old O'Dara, whom I went to see to order some turf, greeted me with these words:

- Did you know that I'm living on my own now ? Not knowing how I should take this, and unaware of what might have happened to his wife, I remained silent, a slightly sad expression on my face, until I was able to muster a questioning “Oh?”

- Yes, she left for London, she’s with my daughter, he said with a smile, and I’m very happy.

Reassured by this news, which had nothing to do with any obituary column, we drank to his new-found celibacy.

My friend Jimmy was in the habit of coming to see me every time the problems with his wife got the better of him, which happened to be often. Trying to soothe their troubles and finding no better reasoning, I finally asked him:

- Do you love your wife?
- No, I love her sister, he said in all seriousness.

I took care to keep my thoughts to myself.

At times, I had no time to work out my reactions. She was blonde, approaching thirty, driving up the boulevard Saint-Germain in her convertible, and had just pulled up at the lights alongside the car where I was a passenger.

- Do you want me to come and hold the plastic duck on the seat next to you? I ventured gaily (I never knew what it was doing there).
- Yes, she said, without another word.

I got in beside her. Fifty metres further she stopped:

- I’d prefer you to drive. Without leaving me any choice in the matter, I found myself at the steering wheel and we took off. For a month we travelled along small Italian roads until we reached Sicily. On the way back I wanted to see Venice which I didn’t know at all.
- I’ll only go to Venice with you if you marry me, she said firmly. I never went to Venice!

Back in Paris, a few weeks later, we were drinking an apéritif in her apartment.

- Since our love is impossible, we will have to kill ourselves.

Then she made for a chest of drawers and took out a revolver. I had just enough time to remain calm. Her determination was evident. Wanting to seize the gun, there followed a struggle on the double bed. Surprised by the strength unleashed by her despair, I redoubled my efforts, managed to get hold of the revolver, and removed the bullets one by one. Having pocketed the ammunition I gave her back the gun. I never saw her again, but I learnt that two months later she had married. I was young and it was quite a story, even without the trip to Venice. Neither did we have time to see Scylla on the Sicilian coast, yet we had time to see Charybdis, in Calabria. But I didn't know that Ithaca was still so far away.

I'll end this overview with a less dramatic story. It's about an eighty-year old man who met a young woman of sixty-seven. They were both widowed. Having experienced the delights of children and grandchildren alike, they found one another, fell in love and, for want of an excuse, declared: "It's wonderful, every moment is precious, because we have so little time left." Before he met her, he had been cursed by rheumatism and could hardly move around, and there he was leaping about joyfully on the arm of his fiancée.

As for myself, at this time, I had remained true to the theories of Charles Fourier [28], but without a phalanstery and on an international scale. I continued to go from one relationship to the next, unable to settle for any one and not wanting to. It was by turning and returning the pivotal love in all directions (in pivotal love, you remain faithful to adultery) that I started to turn. I span round and round, like a spinning top, which turns and turns, and then, like the top I started to whirl, then waver. Then, just like the top, I started to lose my centre, and topple over like the drunkard that I had become.

Without realising it I had now embarked on a long road. I was depressed, so I drank. The more I drank, the more I was depressed. An infernal circle was closing in on me. Every renewed swig of drink brought me that little pink cloud upon which I was trying to achieve a balancing act. Alas, it fell apart quickly enough and I had to start the process all over again. Several friends tried to warn me. I would have none of it: "You're exaggerating, I've only had two glasses of wine."

Then one day, while out for the evening, I saw the person standing behind me reflected in a mirror as he made signs to the person I was speaking to, indicating not to waste his time because I was drunk. It was an unpleasant experience. An old Egyptian poem, over four thousand years ago, had nevertheless sounded a warning :

> "Don't allow yourself to take to drinking beer,
> For when you speak, something else comes out of
> your mouth,
> You don't know who said it,
> You fall over, and your limbs give way beneath you.
> So that they find you on the ground
> Like a small child."
>
> (*The Wisdom of Ani*)

So I drank more in order to forget. Until the day when a friend took me to a meeting of former drinkers. I didn't want to see myself in these men and women, many of whom were visibly marked by their drinking. I listened to them recount episodes of their lives which seemed to have nothing to do with me. I did however acknowledge that after a week of these meetings and no drinking that my face was beginning to resume its normal contours. Physically, I began to feel better. After a few months, having recovered a pleasing form, and feeling as though I was on a rather more solid version of my little pink cloud, I left the group. I clearly had not understood that that was where everything was to begin all over again. Very quickly I found myself spinning hopelessly round and round for a few more years to come.

One November evening, noticing that the bottle of whiskey that I had discreetly purchased in the pub the night before was empty, I decided to go back the very next day and see 'my friends' in Paris. Which is where the greatest journey of my life began. Little by little, as I regained sobriety, I began to understand something. It took me two years of physical sobriety in order to begin to achieve some semblance of mental sobriety, by which I mean seeing life for what it is, without that permanent veil which I so hungered after.

I quickly realised that my story was quite a common one among those other souls who were sobering up. The feeling of emptiness which so often goes hand in hand with depression, this loveless hole, as I call it, or, as in my particular case, this gaping, bottomless *crater*, was what I was filling up with alcohol in order to reduce the emptiness and to erase the sharp edges. I had not yet realised that this *crater* was exactly like the Danaides' barrel, it had to be filled again and again. In many cases, filling it up leads to total destruction. It begins with the loss of your job, your income, then family, friends, home and then "other people don't understand". No, they don't understand. And they cannot understand. All those "get a hold on yourself"'s and "you have no will power" mean nothing. I don't drink because it's what I want, I'm drinking because I haven't found any other way out, I drink because I have to. I'm drinking against my own will. It was in acknowledging that my inner compulsions were stronger than my will that I began to get to the heart of the matter. When I understood that between my will and those traumatic emotions engrained since childhood, that it is always the emotions which gain the upper hand, it was then and only then, that I began to be able to do something. Yet knowing a thing intellectually is not enough.

The only leap possible, in order not to founder completely, having steered a course between two vintages, is to touch the bottom of the *crater* and, with a salutary bound, rise to the surface. In order to do this, only the 'friends' who have lived through such a thing can be of any help to you.
"He who has never lost his footing, never knows how to offer a helping hand" is a lovely expression which shows exactly what I mean.

After a few difficult days, I was able to ride the effects of the physical rupture. If I didn't fill my gaping *crater*, this loveless hole, with alcohol again, then it was still there. What was I to do with something which had always been with me? It was a part of me, and I was used to it even if at times it showed, unwittingly, in my ventriloquist's expression.

The long years that followed my break with alcohol were spent with the need to fill this *crater* with something other than alcohol. In order to achieve this, my 'friends' were there. They helped me to counter reality without shielding its countenance from me. They taught me that my *crater* and I could remain written in stone until death us do part. They taught me that drinking a reassuring glass when faced with a problem will not make my *crater* go away. Which is why I can truly say, with them, that alcoholism is not about having a problem with alcohol! I know that this sentence, taken out of context, must seem absurd. So let's not take it out of context. This notion helped me a great deal. Even now, after many years of sobriety, when a difficulty presents itself, I say to myself: "It's no use having a drink, since that's not going to solve anything." One drink would be one too many because it would bring on the second and then, a thousand drinks would never be enough to fill up the *crater*. Alcoholism is definitely not about alcohol. No more than it is a disease, unless having to fill a *crater* is a disease. Alas, most human beings have a *crater* of one sort or another to fill. They all fill it in their own way. If it isn't alcohol, then it's tobacco, drugs, work, glory or whatever you like, as I've already said.

This is why all strata of society are represented in this brotherhood from hell. This is where I have met state advisors and gangsters, doctors and workers, priests and atheists, policemen and peasants, all wanting to share their experiences in order to help one another and show that it is possible to see life through a new pair of demisted lenses.

The warmth from sharing life's experiences is greater than any social status, which in Ireland at least has no special importance. An Irish singer, very much in vogue, cancelled his duties in order to spend an afternoon with me, because he sensed that I was having a rough time, then phoned me every hour until I came back to the surface. Another person who was taking me back home one night, gave me this simple sentence: "Keep an open mind, and accept that something may help you." As I closed his car door, the depressing slide on which I had found myself, had disappeared.

The magic of words and selfless friendship. For me, it is the cornerstone of the movement. Selfless love for another person. If I, who fell so low, came out of it thanks to *you*, you, candidate for sobriety, you too can come out of it with our help. If you want it enough, then it's possible and we are there. We can help you to find the direction in your life and not go under. This is where I learnt not to rave against things which are independent of me. Cursing the rain will not stop it from falling. On the other hand, taking control over something I can, depends only on me. After that, you must believe in miracles, for I have witnessed them. I do what I can, given what I have; as for the impossible, destiny will take care of that and often rather well.

How many times have I worried myself silly about something that never happened. Today people can say as they like and do as they like and I'll continue along my road. From time to time there will be jeering, arrows, poisoned darts across my path. With a deft wave of the hand I send them off course and they end up in the ditch.

I have also learnt to drop my proverbial intolerance and become more tolerant, even though I confess to its limits, stopping just short of intolerance. I owe all this to 'them'. The whole thing works thanks to their unconditional and selfless friendship. I have a hundred such examples. I will spare you, all except perhaps one: it was the 'friend' who was asked to take a woman back home, someone who wanted to be sober and was in fact totally inebriated. She lived in the outer reaches of the Parisian suburbs. Stretched out on the back seat of his lovely car, he drove her for over an hour, at eleven in the evening, until they reached her house, having passed through the little deserted streets of a deprived quarter. Delighted to have got her safely home without soiling the smart seats of his car, he made off, happy to have done something out of a sense of impartial friendship and without thinking any more of it.

Two years later, at a meeting, a young woman came up to him:

- Do you recognise me? She said.
- No, came the reply.
- About two years ago you took me back home, right out in the suburbs, and since that day I haven't touched a drop of alcohol.

They hadn't known each other. He had done this for her. She existed. Someone had done this for her. Someone had looked after her. Someone had taken the trouble and the time to take her home, to the depths of the suburbs, she who had been rejected by everyone, like the wreck she had in fact become. But if I exist for this man who did this for me, it means that I exist. Thus life may begin again.

This selfless friendship had already been tested by the ancients. Pythagoras' doctrine promoted the idea of close friendship between his followers, founded simply on helping one another. Diodurus of Sicily also tells the story of Clinias who, having learnt that Proros of Cyrene was on his knees, immediately left Italy for Cyrene, taking with him the necessary funds. Yet he had never seen him, it was simply a matter that he was a Pythagorean!

Other stories of this kind are told by Aristoxenus. Such as the one concerning Damon, who agreed to act as guarantor for Pythias, condemned to death, until the latter returned. Pythias came back and the two were pardoned by Dionysius, who was astounded and captivated by such a display of trusting friendship.

A similar story happened during the 1916 Easter Rising in the Post Office in Dublin. After five days of fighting, the building was eventually taken by the British army. A suspect who had been apprehended, denied being in the opposing party; something which would have condemned him to death. A rebel came forward and confirmed that the suspect had not been in the building, as he himself had been. Following this affirmation, it was the latter who was condemned to death and shot.

This unconditional friendship, or shall we say, love of truth and mutual help, reminds us of course of another: that of maternal love. This too is unconditional, totally disinterested, and for this a woman will give her life for her child. But I would advance a note of caution, for maternal love can become a suffocating weight in certain cases. Something which was never the case with those 'friends' who are not emotionally involved. It is an act of unconditional love in the sense that they are doing it for another person. There is no bartering. They do it because they feel like it, for the pleasure of giving freely, for the pleasure of giving as they have been given to.

This is one of the reasons why the family of an alcoholic can never help him, because the emotional attachment gets in the way, and that's without going into the manipulation which is always possible, whether consciously or unconsciously. In many cases the family is often annoyed at seeing this band of "drunkards" succeed in helping others to give up drink where they themselves had failed.

Be that as it may, this non-emotional and disinterested love proffered by our 'friends' is linked to the mother. Just as problems with drug abuse are often linked to the father. In French the verb *biberonner* means literally both to give the bottle to a baby and to booze... and Gore Vidal referred to his brandy, not without irony, as his "mother's milk."

Among the hundreds of testimonies that I have heard, I have always been struck by the large number of those people who have experienced a lack of maternal love, often, though not always, arising in infancy. Take for example the young man who, having remained sober for five years, began his story with these words: "I began to drink on the day of my mother's funeral, I was twenty-eight years old" and concluded with the following: "I don't know why I began to drink." The *crater* can beckon at any age.

Another fifty-five year old woman began to drink when her husband left her for a younger woman. She ended her life in bed with a bottle of whiskey. Alcoholism is definitely not a problem of alcohol. It's a gaping hole of love which we fill up with alcohol. Neither is it a problem of will power. I don't 'want' to drink. My feelings push me to it.

The absence of maternal love, that same *crater*, may sometimes find a substitute in either the love which artists believe to be bestowed upon them by the public, or the power given to politicians. They are often seen, once this acclaim has been taken away from them, to turn to alcohol for salvation. There are many examples of this.

The case of Eliot Ness is even more striking. This legendary police officer who rose to fame during the Prohibition whilst fighting a merciless battle against alcohol, in fact ended his days as an alcoholic. He died unacknowledged and defeated. Forty years after his death, his inheritors, too impoverished to maintain his urn, had the ashes of this "incorruptible" person disposed of. If even the *ayatollahs* succumb, then perhaps the problem really is elsewhere.

One could consider the problem from another angle, for example those who stop drinking with the help of medical aids and detoxification cures. They fall back into their old ways all too quickly. One of our 'friends' told us that he had been through seventy-four detoxification programmes. No sooner had he come out than he buried himself in the first pub he could find and made up for lost time. What do you do with an empty *crater* when there is nothing left to put in it, except fill it up with alcohol. Even psychotropic medicines only delay the solution, which is how I myself went back to drinking, after a few months of sobriety and my first attempt to give up. In the same way that after an operation one doesn't feel the pain straight away because of the anaesthetic, then little by little one is reconnected with one's body and the pain. It's the same with alcohol, when its anaesthetising effect wears off, we feel the emptiness of the crater which rears its head anew.

If, after many years, I have managed to tend to my *crater* without turning to alcohol, then it is because I have found other substitutes. Tobacco being one of them. I started smoking again when I stopped drinking. And I am no less happy for it. For tobacco, as harmful and addictive as it may be, does not alter one's behaviour. It does not shield me from life's reality, which I now manage to confront whatever the obstacles. They are many, but I can now put them in their rightful place.

Many associations have been founded on the same basis of shared difficulties. The driving force that comes from the void of suffering can be of great sustenance to others. There are associations which provide support for people with cancer, the near and dear of suicide cases, compulsive spenders, sex maniacs, kleptomaniacs, workaholics, and many others that I cannot recall. There is, however, one important one missing: that which deals with political and religious rigidity. This is an almost insurmountable undertaking. Like the neighbour who, upon opening her door to two Jehovah's witnesses, came up with this retort: "If I don't even believe in my own religion, which is after all the only real one, how on earth do you expect me to believe in yours!"

All these addictions arise from one and the same thing: trying to satisfy or fill that gaping hole. That empty, invisible yet ever-present *crater*. All those title holders of the many diverse addictions are often proud of the fact that they neither smoke nor drink. They don't know that they are just playing out another version of the same thing and that their addictions are often more harmful when they become *ayatollahs*.

It was after I had found a certain level of physical sobriety that I decided to open up my cottage as a B&B. The decision was not easy. How would I who had come in search of solitude, reconcile this with a stream of visitors. The need to earn a living decided the matter. I had no choice. As so often in life, necessity proved to be my salvation. Life throws up more imagination than we ourselves at times, and in allowing it to do so we find ourselves the better for it, if only we accept what is presented to us. What was presented to me has surpassed my wildest dreams. The pleasure of receiving guests of every age, nationality and occupation, provides a window on the world which never fails to satisfy my insatiable curiosity. My encounters with both men and women who kindly pay me a visit, more than fulfill me, especially when they show their appreciation for the place that I have created. If they find themselves at one with my creation and the spirit which pervades here, then we almost certainly will have things in common which we may lose no time in exploring. When they leave, they demonstrate their friendship, declaring: "Your cottage is difficult to find, but even more difficult to leave." I would like to take this opportunity to thank them for the warmth and friendship which they have shown me.

One rainy, windy January evening a young couple came running up to my doorway. Already soaked through by the rain which fell as they made their way from the car to my cottage, I settled them in front of the turf fire, which filled the fireplace with its pungent odour, when suddenly the man upbraided me, saying:

- You're mad to live here all alone!
- I'm not alone, I replied; you are here.

I am well aware that this is just another way of filling my *crater*. The Danaides' barrel is sometimes replaced by the Naiades who come looking for comfort and help me, for a while, to fill the bottomless *crater*.

On the advice of friends who had already stayed with me, a couple from Durban who were going through a difficult patch, decided to come and spend two days in my home. "After two days over there, you will see life differently," they told them. Having made the two eleven hour flights, a week later I received a message from South Africa thanking me for their refound serenity "I rediscovered my soul" the woman added.

Having arrived late one evening, two French couples left the following morning after breakfast. We exchanged the usual pleasantries that pass between me and my guests. Two weeks later I was surprised to receive a letter of thanks bearing these words from one of the young women: "I often think of you and your corner of paradise, and this helps me to give a sense to my own life at the moment. Just by closing my eyes I can see that strange calm, that peaceful serenity which emanates from you. These images help me each time I need to overcome my anxiety. Something which I thought impossible to resolve, took a new direction on the day we visited you, as though your aura had helped me to grow. I know now that I can draw back the curtains and find myself facing out to sea, or into the wind, even a storm, or the sun, but also facing life, in a mist of tears, or else bathed in rays of joy. And this I think I owe to you and to the charm of your cottage."

I received no further news. I say that I was surprised, because we exchanged nothing in particular, either spoken or implicit. Perhaps she had glimpsed the eye of the ventriloquist. Perhaps she had understood what I was saying from within. Perhaps she had seen in the expression in my eyes those things I had no need to say. Perhaps she had heard that which I did not say. At times the unspoken core doesn't do so badly. That unspoken part of me and my self were working away together in spite of me.

A fifty-five year old Parisian engineer, having spent a few days at my place, sent me the following letter: "I can honestly say to you that I spent three of the happiest days of my life in your home. This is the door through which we pass into the world of dreams. It's Cocteau's mirror, the well in Alice in Wonderland, Joyce's tower. Céline wrote: *lie or die, you have to choose*, but you have managed to make Céline lie, something few have achieved."

As gratifying and full of heartfelt friendship as they are, these messages are not enough to cement the bottom of the *crater*. This is something which can only be done from within. That little bush growing inside us through childhood and which is full of vital strength, of mischievous, fun-loving energy, ready to burst out laughing after every prankish joke, was spreading its infectious joy. This strong little bush whose leaves were ready to burst forth, was poking through the blonde curls. This hardy little bush, with its tender green blush provoked a sort of perpetual gaiety. This little bush which had yet to learn what ventriloquy was. This little bush still didn't know that its young shoots, which asked only to grow, would be ripped apart, like wisps of straw, by an engine of death which had come to darken the blue sky of his carefree childhood. Since that day, there has always been a dark shadow at the bottom of the crater which is reflected, immeasurable, in spite of the vast expanse of blue sky.

It was the adult that I became who was in fact left to tend this little bush, again and again as it struggles at times to withstand the sudden storms. Its canopy, strengthened by successive cuttings, successfully confronts the ups and downs of everyday life. At times even with increased serenity when faced with life-turning events.

But not always. The little bush sometimes reappeared, stunted, devoid of its delightfully vibrant, vital and energy-enhancing creativity. That little bush which had been shut in a cellar by a cantankerous aunt, because of a few mischievous pranks that my brother and I must have got into. How can a little bush flourish in a cellar? It can only suffocate and languish. I finally found a way out. I was four years old and my brother barely older: "We can't stay here, we have to leave," I said. The sun was well on its way down, for the shadow of the two little boys was long enough for me to still remember it today. This shadow, which went before us on the long track must have been of some reassurance, for we walked for a long time. Our house had disappeared in the distance, when I saw the plumes of dust raised by my father's car as he came looking for us.

It had been the only way out that I could think of. I was less frightened by the unknown terrain and the jackals that roamed there, than by my own house. This mechanism still operates from time to time. Faced with an unbearable situation, my desire to leave takes on an uncontrollable force, drawing from the roots of that little tenacious bush. The wise and self-composed adult, charged with calming it, is at pains to win him over, to cajole, reassure, take him by the hand and show him along the path where those childhood fears are no longer necessary. It's not a matter of controlling them, but of accepting them. For control itself can become a drug. Like all drugs it can become compulsive. If we fail to control the uncontrollable, we experience it as a personal failure. So I let life carry me on out of control. The energy which is liberated as a result, allows me to perceive each ray of sun, every tit and every chaffinch competing for a few peanuts… and each new guest as he arrives.

I have met some wonderful people who have confided in me their hopes and their disappointments in life. We have conversed as friends in front of the turf fire. Christopher, the house robin appears from time to time at the window to take a piece of bread, which is sometimes too heavy for his little wings, or rather for the protruding stomach of a well-fed bird. Or else, presented with a sunset which has lit up the heather-covered hills, my guests, stunned by such a wealth of beauty, found themselves unable to utter a word. And there we remained, motionless, silently savouring the moment as it stretched into infinity.

It was summer when a couple arrived: he was around fifty, a film director. She was a stunning young starlet. An underlying conflict caused them to ask me for a room each. Having only one room left, I told them that that would be difficult. Finally, they agreed to share the same room. The next morning, rising early, I crossed the garden. The man was sleeping in his car, his head resting on the steering wheel. I slipped away discreetly. After having reassured me that he had slept well, he was unable to eat a thing during breakfast. I said to myself - he's my best customer; he sleeps in his car and won't eat breakfast. I could have a hundred customers a day like him. All I would need is a huge car park! Such was not the case. The disagreement resolved itself, they stayed five days, loved the setting, their room and the breakfast…

A couple who had been living together for eight years and who had two children, decided to get married. They organised a party at my house. On returning to London, the young bride phoned me in order to thank me: "Do you know what my four-year old son said to me? - Mummy, you should get married again, I want to go back to Paul's house."

A little five-year old girl declared: "Paul, I like your breakfast, but I would prefer to have it in bed." Life is going to be difficult for that adorable little doll.

From a pair of lovers whom I asked whether they were married, came the reply: "Yes, but not to each other!"

I have received several letters inviting me to a wedding for which I was deemed in some way responsible, as the proposal had been prompted by the romantic setting of this place which, they said, would remain forever engraved in their minds.

Another letter thanked me as follows: "Thanks to your idyllic place, the complete calm, your romantic cottage, I realised that this was not the man for me."

I always ask my guests what their profession is. To this question, one of them replied: "I am a funeral director." He regaled me with some amusing anecdotes about his work with the dead, such as this one: arriving in front of a church, he opened the rear hatch of the hearse and realised he had forgotten the coffin. He had some difficulty trying to convince them that he had taken the wrong vehicle. Daily contact with death, presented in the form of inert corpses, had had no psychological effect on him, he reassured me, except that it's impossible for him to visit Madame Tussaud's. "It makes my blood go cold," he said. "When I took my children a few years ago, I wanted only one thing: to get out." After a few days in my house he said to me "Paul, I love this room where we have breakfast. On my desk I've got a little ceramic coffin which was there in my father's time and my grandfather's before him. It's a very quaint old object. I'd like you to have it, so I'll send it to you. I did indeed receive it. It takes pride of place on my mantelpiece, to remind us that we are all mortal.

From conception to death, all phases of life pass through my home. Christenings, proposals of marriage, divorces, weekends which hail either a separation or a love tryst. Often all at the same time with no ill effect. When the above-mentioned undertaker was staying here, I had a customer who was ill. I took the liberty of saying: "You'd be as well to get better because I have a funeral director here at the moment and he's just waiting for your health to deteriorate." It worked. She quickly recovered.

On another occasion, I found a rosary under a bed. I have never been able to identify the sinner who committed her soul to God instead of her body.

A young British couple: she was a doctor and he a policeman. Over breakfast, somewhat embarrassed, she asked me what was the correct position for using the bidet. My first reaction, as a helpful sort of person, was to offer a practical lesson. Her husband's profession decided me otherwise.

He was bodyguard to a minister. The latter was dining with his mistress in a restaurant when a quarrel took a nasty turn and the minister was at pains to protect himself from being walloped by the woman's handbag. The bodyguard was obliged to use his considerable bulk to put an end to the hostilities.

A very rotund couple were on their honeymoon. She asked me at breakfast what I did all day. After they left I found the bed broken in two. I spent the afternoon mending it, whilst muttering to myself - "And what do you do all day?"

A young woman descended on me at the crack of dawn, wearing next to nothing, to tell me that her husband was sleeping and that the bathroom tap was not working. Freud would have relished the symbolism, but he would have been mistaken. She was no nymphomaniac, but simply a tease looking as though butter wouldn't melt in her mouth.

A yachtsman felt the urge to tell me that before crossing the Atlantic, he stopped in Senegal for eight days, as he was obliged to take on necessary provisions for his trip. Various young people were making their way around the sailing boats offering their services as shipmates for the trip. Ok, he said to one of them, but first of all you have to help me load the boat. After a week of shifting crates of water and other provisions, the yachtsman stuck his fingers up at him and set sail. How could anyone boast such lowly conduct?

Some people are jinxed, too; I have borne witness to them. One lady customer managed within a few hours, to blow up the water heater, the heating and then the bedside lamp.

A high court judge explained to me that he didn't read his case notes. He preferred to observe the "body language" of the accused. It's the first time they've been listened to and they just want to be finally heard; then they exist and the sentence becomes secondary. Said he…

I offer promotional lighters to my smoking clients. For the non-smokers I have empty ones, telling them that "It's never too late to start." Then a cardiologist who was a smoker went one better: he gave me a splendid lighter before leaving…

Faced with having to iron a shirt for my young son, an Italian woman who came every year from Venice, offered to do it for me. I declined the offer and her husband insisted: “Let her do it, she can’t stand seeing a man work.” The next day an American woman asked me to iron her dress. The moral being: it’s better to marry an Italian woman than an American one.

An Irish man was unable to tolerate a picture not hanging completely straight on his wall. He resolved the problem by leaving one of his pictures in a very obviously crooked position. Whenever anyone called this to his attention, he replied: “That’s how I like it.”

Another person felt compelled to check three times to see if his door was properly locked. His solution was simple: he stopped locking his door.

An enormous Mercedes drove up my little drive. It put me in mind of some sort of “have you seen me” which had got lost. Not a bit of it. Having arrived in Dublin on the second of January, all the small cars had already been hired for the end of year festivities. This was the only one left. The driver was Gabriele Salvatores, a simple man, if ever there was one and in spite of the Oscar he won for his film, *Mediterranean*. We spent several happy days dissecting Italian cinema, whilst cursing his enormous car which prevented him from exploring so many little Irish roads.

It was summer, about six o’clock in the morning. The sound of cattle lowing woke the whole household. A herd of cows had invaded the lawn, blithely tearing it up with their heavy hooves. I asked my customers to help drive them back onto the road. Several young women in knickers came out to give me a hand, placing themselves at strategic points about the lawn. The scene was delightful.

A printer offered to redesign my business cards for the B&B, at no charge to myself. He found my cards unprofessional. So I allowed a professional to take over. A few weeks later, I received five thousand cards whereon the photograph had been printed upside down. I nevertheless had to thank him for his professional services, without drawing his attention to the blunder.

Every 28th April the cuckoo comes back to occupy some trees around my cottage. He comes above all with the intention of wreaking havoc in the existing nests. After the first night an English man came and told me how thrilled he was to hear the cuckoo's unmistakable cry, something he hadn't heard since childhood. But after the second night, he came into the room with quite another story: "Paul, I'm fed up with this cuckoo; from five o' clock in the morning onwards his incessantly loud 'cuckoo' stops me from sleeping…" "The most amazing thing of all", declared another couple, "is that the guests in the adjoining room have brought an alarm clock with a cuckoo chime." I had some difficulty convincing them otherwise.

Finding me somewhat tired, a thoughtful Canadian guest sent me some vitamin pills along with her thankyou note. She recommended that I take one tablet every day in order to restore my good health. A year later I received a call from the very same Canadian lady who enquired as to whether I had indeed taken my vitamins. I replied rather evasively that I had taken them and that my health was excellent and that I appreciated her concern. I couldn't have been more mistaken!

- You should never have taken them, she said, completely panic-struck, I have just read in a magazine that those vitamins are carcinogenic…

I tried my best to reassure her, saying I hadn't taken very many and that I was in excellent health, with or without the vitamins…

The lawn which surrounds my cottage had just been cut, thanks to the boundless energy of the wild rabbits which darted back and forth in every direction. I occasionally had to run over the grass with a mower to level out the patches of weeds which had failed to tempt them. An engineer who taught maths in a well-known French school asked me whether the grass always remained at the same height or whether I had to cut it. "From time to time I cut it with a helicopter which I fly upside down," was the only answer I could summon.

An American woman whose appearance more than belied her sixty years, staying on her own, came in for breakfast complaining that there was only one chair in her room: "It's a room for two people, so there should be two chairs." In spite of the absurdity of her objection, I came back quickly enough with the following reply:

There were two chairs, but since you reserved the room for one person, I took one away. I told the story to an Irish friend, saying that I had sometimes, though only occasionally, rather stupid guests. He replied:

- No, Paul, God bless them. What a poor life they have.

I learnt a lesson that day; in fact what a poor life they must endure!

The only remaining bed was a divan in the library. My Irish guest made good use of the room. "The advantage of sleeping in this room, he said the next day, is that when you wake up you feel more intelligent..."

I was explaining to one of my guests how to find my house. You'll see a sign with the name of the town on the main road. Turn right and follow the road. He got lost. Two hours later, he turned up.

- Didn't you see the sign on the main road?
- Oh, yes, I saw the sign, he said, but I myself don't like to turn off main roads!

When I ask the question: "What do you do?" I sometimes get the reply: "civil servant." I can then only ask which domain: "Tax or police?" It is invariably either one or the other. When the tax inspector paid me the next morning, I had to restrain myself from remarking that it was an agreeable change to receive money, rather than a bill, from him…

A visitor found himself lost on a little road and asked the way.

- You aren't lost, replied the man, you're in Ireland.

If from time to time we fail to lose our way, then we are unlikely to ever find our true path.

On another occasion, I asked the same question of a police woman's son.

- I'm a researcher at the University of Philadelphia.
- What sort of research? I enquired.
- I do research on the testicles of fruit flies, came the reply.

This is how I discovered that the DNA of flies is very close to that of human beings. An Irish woman to whom I told this story, replied:

- Proof that beauty is to be found in the smallest of things!

To the same question a Scottish woman replied that she was doing research in a laboratory.

- What kind of research? I asked with interest.
- We import foreskins from Israel in order to make a cream to soothe the varicose veins of old women.

Since you are now used to it, I'm going to make another little digression, because this business of foreskins is not without significance. That they provide relief for ulcers on the legs of old women is not so surprising. In fact, Henry V was already convinced of the properties of Christ's Holy foreskin to enhance his wife's fertility. To this end, the foreskin thief had to choose between 21 supposed foreskins, all claimed to be *the* one by the same number of abbeys. In 1422 he threw in his lot with the one from Chartres, which had been authenticated as being the original one by Pope Clément VII. The monks of Chartres had great difficulty in retrieving the Holy item, which was the subject of so much envy! I myself had always naively believed that the pilgrims made their way to Chartres in order to admire the architecture of the cathedral. [29]

As for Catherine of Sienna, [30] it was said that she wore on her finger one of the numerous 'real' foreskins, in order to symbolise her mystical marriage to Christ. It has to be said that she was preceded by another mystic, Agnès Blannbekin, an Austrian nun from the tertiary order of Franciscans (d. 1315) who, in the course of her religious ecstasies, felt the presence of the Holy foreskin in her mouth. [31] Lacan has already written about the link between female sexual pleasure and the ecstasies of the mystics. But on this occasion I feel that even Lacan has been surpassed... by the effects of circumcision, in itself symbolic of castration! I end my digression here, for what it is worth, and come back to my guests.

A couple in their fifties. He is tall, slim, elegant. I ask my other guests at breakfast:

- What do you think his job is?

One of them suggests:

- University Professor.

Someone else:

- Professor of Medicine.

When our man eventually appeared for his breakfast, I put the habitual question to him:

- Me, he replied in a relaxed manner, I sell panties! We spent a long time around the old table from Auvergne, talking about this fascinating subject.

All the guests of the groom had come to sleep at my place. I learnt that the couple had an eight month-old baby. Before the wedding, the groom came to greet all his friends:

- What do you think I heard – that you already have a baby before getting married. Does the bishop know?
- The bishop has one too, was his reply.

Two young Irish couples were discussing family matters at breakfast one day. The eighteen-year old younger brother of one of the couples was saying how he had had the difficult job of telling his mother that his seventeen-year old girlfriend was pregnant.

- That's wonderful, said his mother, I love children, that's life, it's fantastic. We'll help you, don't worry, etc. Then, after a silence: And Dad will be thrilled, he was so afraid you were homosexual!

As for myself, since seeing a photo of Oscar Wilde's wife, I would gladly have become a homosexual. Not having it to hand, especially on those evenings that were so very long, cold, dark and windy, when all was howling outside, I would put on a record to listen to some opera, more or less loud, depending on whatever emotion I happened to be feeling.

That evening it was in the warm and powerful voice of Cathy that I sought solace. Yes, the one from *Wuthering Heights*, the one who would have saved Don Juan by becoming the one thousand and fourth. But Don Juan cannot be saved. Listening to those sultry voices which go to your very soul I came to understand, when I had my music bookshop, why so many homosexuals were captivated by the voices of divas and constantly asked me for recordings and photographs of these formidable women.

Revered by the media, the great, all-powerful *cailín* was the incarnation of the mother, and reassured the little boy who no longer needed to hide, in order to admire the glorious sceptre. The jewels of La Castafiore are always stolen, since they do not exist. The father may exist, but they refuse him the right to carry the sceptre. The Mother, the all-powerful *cailín*, is invested with power if the Father is absent or else insignificant and unable to prevent junior from believing him, from believing her, from being impressed.

There are many examples in literature: Ravel and his excessive love for his mother. He appears to have had no sexual dalliances, neither homosexual nor heterosexual. He had his music instead. There is no more erotic music than his! Jouhandeau declared, at ninety-two years of age: "My mother! There is not one woman to match her." Barthes placed his mother very high: "I think back with a terrible wrench, at mother's last words: "My Roland, My Roland!"

I have always been shocked on hearing grown-ups, some of them quite advanced in years, referring to their mothers as 'Mummy'. It seemed very infantile to me. Perhaps my past has something to do with it. It must be said that they have had some literary support: the first words of Albert Camus' novel, *The Outsider*, are: "Mummy died today." And Proust, in the first pages of *In Search of…*, tells us how: "My only consolation when I went up to prepare for the night, was that Mummy would come and kiss me when I was in bed."

As for Sappho of Lesbos, who gave her name to Sapphism and to lesbians, it is well known that twenty-six centuries ago, she roamed Greece from Asia Minor, looking for her "shepherd" who had abandoned her. Unable to find him, she threw herself from the top of the Leucade promontory. Not so long ago, the inhabitants of Lesbos asked the authorities to change the name of their island, finding it too sexually loaded. Their request was dismissed. Feminists too often refer to men. This shouldn't be said, however, as they don't like it.

The eye of the ventriloquist has the advantage of being able to recognize, thanks to its *crater*, feminine criteria. Of course, it will always be subjective. This *crater* will be so powerful, so seductive, that it will become the criteria for love itself. Even the most beautiful small of the back, the most enchanting eyes on earth, will be of no use before the *crater*. The emblems of femininity may rise up where we least expect them. It is only through the eye of the ventriloquist that they may be discerned, sometimes named, but rarely viewed in an objective light. As for those emblems of femininity which are regularly seen in magazines and advertising, these are purely deceptive. Models who know perfectly well how to arouse desire when they are suitably adorned, find themselves devoid of this power once they are stripped of their regalia. The slimmer and slinkier they are, the more the couturier and the hair stylist are free to create *their* vision. Which goes to show that desire is set in motion by that extra something which does not really exist. This is why women call upon the best experts in the subject: homosexual hairdressers and couturiers; masters in the art of deception, these evasive experts in shifting chiffon, whose whole art rests on denying that there is anything to hide.

Every morning from my hills, which are certainly no deception, I admired the valley before me. Sometimes a few clouds of mist floated this way and that, above the sodden fields. Not a day passed when I was not in awe of this spectacle. The soothing atmosphere came perhaps from the cattle which were grazing peacefully down below, near the gate, or perhaps from the clouds, delicately tinged with mauve by the reflection of the sun over the sea. The sometimes strong wind failed to drown the sound of the waterfall which tumbled down the fields behind my cottage. This waterfall had over time hollowed out a small cave, rather like that of Lourdes, a photograph of which can be seen next to the Pope, hung over many Irish fireplaces.

One winter evening, at the time when my boundless imagination was still nourished and exacerbated by Guinness, I was in the little pub crammed full of old objects and hundreds of jugs of every size and description hanging from the ceiling, surrounded by the warm company of the regular customers, my taste for derision caused some unease, when I announced through the wafts of smoke:

- This morning at dawn, as I often do, I went walking across the fields. Passing by my grotto, I was amazed to see the Virgin Mary. I suppose you realize that thanks to this apparition, the glittering silver of my river will now change to gold. In fact, the water will be endowed with miraculous powers and I could serve it by the glass. The resulting fame will bring thousands of coach loads of pilgrims to the town. Even if they're not all Irish they'll drink more than just water, miraculous or not. Your pub will become the most famous in the world and the whole area will enjoy prosperity for years to come.

The sceptical smile of my audience told me quickly enough that however many empty glasses there were on the table, the joking stopped at the doors of the Church.

Not wanting to be defeated, encouraged by a few more pints of Guinness, I went on:

- I've got another idea: I'll build a ski slope on the hills which run down to the village. With artificial snow right up to the pub door. The royal mile for my clients, who will of course become yours. There'll be an international airport for jumbo airplanes. You can sell your fields to hotel developers. Thousands of American tourists will come and buy your Aran sweaters directly from your homes, so that you'll no longer need to export them.

At this point everyone reacted. It took me a few minutes to understand that it was not my flights of fancy that had caused the kneejerk reaction. No, it was simply the idea of an invasion of Americans which made them shudder. The wild imaginings of the *Frenchman* would change nothing. Even though green is the colour of Ireland, the green note is not king in these parts.

I stood a round for everyone in order to free up new idea:

- I've got a better idea: that old hearse which is rotting away in Malachy's field, I'll buy it and turn it into an ice cream van and sell ice creams on the beaches. Seated in place of the coffin, I could serve several people at once. What is more, in the evening, I can park my venerable vehicle in front of the pub and there'll be something in it for everyone.

This new idea left them unmoved. Realising in spite of the late hour and the heady emanations of alcohol in the air, that more than one family member of those present must have made his last journey in this vehicle, the idea wasn't in the best of taste.

Old Danny, who was normally happy to just smoke his pipe by the fire, came to my rescue.

- Paul, he said in a warm voice, since you've such a lot of ideas, we should make you president of Ireland. An Irishman [32] was president of France, now it's the turn of a Frenchman to be president of this country.
- I agree, I said, on condition that I can ride down O' Connell Street standing on a motorcycle surrounded by four limousines.

I don't remember how the evening ended. Perhaps I was taken home by four limousines.

Even though I stopped drinking a long time ago, I still like to spend an odd evening in the warm little pub and I still manage to throw out some wild ideas which inevitably shake people up. Now that I have my head back, I no longer need alcohol to respond with a slightly subversive reply to the dry and ever-generous witticisms of the Irish. One of the charms of the Irish pub is the absence of social class. The lawyer shares time with the local electrician, the doctor comes down for an evening with the mechanic, the bank manager with the carpenter. It's the same for the different age groups. Young girls can share a table with their grandmothers and burst out laughing at the same jokes. Old and young discuss all manner of subjects in an uncomplicated way. Young Brian accosted me one evening between two whiskeys:

- Paul, yesterday evening a young French woman was asking for your address. She asked me if I had your phone number. So I gave her mine…

The warm conviviality which reigns in these places is never tarred by religious leanings, financial or political positions, nor even qualifications which are never referred to. Life is always so much more important than the rest. Even the *Gardaí* (Police) are friendly. They are there to help solve problems and not to create them. France is one of the rare countries where qualifications have so much importance. Between the time they are awarded and one's death, they lay strung out after the name of the deceased in the death columns. The poor deceased is hounded by a list of diplomas and decorations. The serious enumeration of these ancient scraps of parchment simply serve as pious entreaty to enter the kingdom of God. This derisory list always made me smile, as I thought of all those little worms who would certainly gain much more enjoyment at consuming a highly qualified supper. As for me, I would rather be buried alongside Baudelaire so that I can make full use of his well-versed worms.

Here in Ireland, qualifications do not figure in the death columns, but a list of the places where the deceased lived, does. The French have a habit of informing you, in a supposedly casual way, of their university careers: "I met my wife at the Trinity ball." Very often in the first few minutes after they have been introduced. It doesn't matter whether you have qualifications or not, what really counts is that you have prestigious ones, because then you can play at being prestigious. You are no longer Mr. Smith who was "at Oxford" - you will become an Oxford graduate whose name is Mr. Smith.

Graduating from one of the *Grandes Ecoles* is not a crime, but wanting to go to one is.

Like that businessman who didn't do so well in business and who, after every disaster, wrote yet another book on how to succeed. He is always holding forth in the media headlines, going on about his qualifications.

Wanting to go to one of the *Grandes Ecoles* means wanting to aim for an often prestigious career, but it rarely means engaging in real life. Faced with the unforeseen twists and turns of life, no qualification will serve as an escape route… Just when they thought they were well and truly on track, life can suddenly send you off on a wrong turning, or, when they don't realise that they are stuck on a track which ends in a cul-de-sac, like those parallel lines extending into infinity.

The role of the father, who obliges his son to follow a certain path, is often a deciding factor in these choices. Whatever his own path may have been, or whatever his unfulfilled goal, either way the son isn't left much room to manoeuvre. He'll do what his father wants. This is why whole progeny find themselves sitting in the same seat as their father. Those same children, once embarked on that path, find themselves securely behind the paternal locomotive, with their only luxury being a certain secure lifestyle. The calling card, for these specialists in generalities, will be the astonishment of the general public when then see that they have paralysed the economy. Should such a situation befall me, then I would consider that I had failed to educate my offspring properly.

It's a business card which, far from being a start in life, is an end in itself; one which you feel obliged to proffer at every little event in order to feel that you exist. This is what some French doctors do to me when they reserve a room: "I'm Dr. so and so." I invariably reply that I am full. The best of all was when a wife said: "My husband is a doctor and I would like the most expensive room." I managed to convince her that she should look for somewhere closer to her requirements.

This business card, with which the well-qualified person draws attention to himself, resembles one of those veils that naked women use to draw attention to their naked bodies. The qualification is the veil of nudity and it is presented because there is nothing behind it. The quality of the veil is to make us feel that that nakedness is well-protected. But it is not the quality of the cloth that makes the man. At times it is even quite the contrary; the business card of some highly-qualified person, such as were sometimes shown to me by customers in my bookshop, served only as the glittering backdrop to their stupidity. You can have qualifications up to the armpits and have the mind of a crossword buff!

Here in Ireland, qualifications take their rightful place. Parents try their best first to make men and women out of their children, then to help them to gain qualifications, even high level qualifications, but, in every instance this eventuality takes second place. Here a qualification is not worn as a banner, much as a Christian wears a cross. It is simply one extra thing.

A contrario, I could name numerous heads of industry, designers, writers, politicians who rarely possess high level qualifications in their field. These men are driven by something else, by a much more powerful engine than a piece of paper, by a force which arises from a depth of desire which has many origins. The profound desire to create will be given better and freer reign for not having been 'yoked' to a minefield of theories.

As a student of philosophy at the Sorbonne, a young teacher told us at the beginning of the year: "Remember, the lessons are not simply here for you to come to every single one, and that your work consists of four hours of concentration, ten minutes reading and one mark." I replied that I was not there for that. When I ran into her a few months later in the seething streets of Saint-Germain in May 68, she greeted me by my name, and remarked that she was surprised to no longer see me in her class. I reminded her that since the lessons were not there simply to go to, I had started by skipping hers first. As for myself, I was surprised to see her there, since she seemed to embody quite the opposite of the spirit of May 68. Culture is neither a diploma nor a mark. A few decades later, she was still to be heard holding forth on the radio. I have just heard her by chance replying to a journalist who introduced her as the daughter of a woman who ran a pharmacy. No, she replied, my mother was the pharmacist. A pharmacy store holder is the one who looks after the shop, my mother was a qualified pharmacist. So, continued the journalist with humour, your mother was both pharmacist and pharmacy store owner. Very good. My diagnosis as a student was still short of the mark! I had refused to be 'yoked' to the mould of the *rue des Ecoles*.

Then, culture took the upper hand over artifice. Culture is the sun which lights up my nights, making them more beautiful than the greyest of days. The pursuit of culture comes before all notion of economics. The right to enjoy culture is not a right to work, and the qualified person has the right to be unemployed.

When I was still a young man, a friend who was a teacher in a business school, finding himself unable to take a class one day, asked me to fill in at short notice.

- I have never taught a lesson in my life, I said, let alone business studies.

- Never mind, he replied, if no-one replaces me, I'll get the sack. So tell them about your experiences in England.

There's no price on friendship, so I did as asked.

Arriving one hour early, I walked around the block for three quarters of an hour. To lend some support, a black briefcase dangled from my hand, damp with worry. When I finally found myself alone with the forty or so students, I began my 'lesson':

- I was given the task by a French company, of establishing a sales outlet in Great Britain. In each region I had to find an agent who would sell the public works machinery that we produced: excavators and tower cranes. When I arrived in London, I looked for the biggest company that might use this sort of machinery. Having tracked down one of them, based in Cornwall and employing eight thousand people, I called them:
- I'd like to speak to the manager, I said.
- Which one? Replied a charming voice, the senior manager?
- Well yes, I replied in a firm voice.
- Ah, he's busy, just a minute... I'll put you through to the Company Director.

In Anglo-Saxon countries it's a lot easier to speak to company directors than in France, where a secretary who is rather too full of herself, often puts up a wall of routine questions: "Could I ask what the subject is?" To which I reply by a disarming and firm: "It's to speak to him."

The lovely voice put me through to the Company Director. Not wanting to lose time in Cornwall, which was an eight-hour train ride away, and having given my name, I suggested the following:

- I have come from Paris and I am calling you from London. I would like to see you and there is a train which would get me to Cornwall at 3 o'clock and another which will take me back to London at 5 o'clock. Could you see me between 3 and 5 p.m?

- Sir, he replied, no-one has ever made a return trip from London just for two hours, so it would be hard not to accept.

When I arrived in the little town, the Director himself was waiting for me at the station with his chauffeur and large saloon.

- Since you're making a sixteen-hour trip in order to see me, I could hardly do otherwise, he said in a friendly voice.

He ordered eight machines from me. And that is how I found my way into the British market.

'My' students looked on open-mouthed at my rather unorthodox approach.

Then one of them said:

- Obviously it's easy for you; you look so at ease and sure of yourself!

It's true he had not seen me pacing around the school, feeling very unsure, before 'my' lesson.

Yet it's not such a contradiction. When I don't have any choice, I confront things with incredible ease.

When I was doing my military service, I used to leave the base, dressed in civilian clothing, without permission, every week-end, and without ever being caught. I had already accepted the eight days prison which would be imposed, were I found out. Every time there was a check, out of solidarity, someone, often someone I didn't even know, would reply that I was in the infirmary, on watch, or on a mission. This 'luck' that my friends thought must be due to some sort of special protection from a General, was simply a question of attitude. I accepted the consequences. I was ready to go to prison on Monday morning. Having accepted this certainty, I felt completely free and walked past the guard-room with disconcerting ease, something which has always served me well. During the twenty-six months I had to serve in the army I never once went to prison. There was only one occasion when, as I made for the guard room dressed in civilian clothing, one Thursday at midday, an officer from the top of the steps leading up to the guard room, called out at me "Halt there, where are you going?" I didn't reply to his injunction, but headed towards the sentry and said firmly, showing him my driving licence: "Salute me as though I were an officer." He clicked his heels together while saluting me and I walked past the guard room trying to look as relaxed as possible. This was the closest I came to prison.

I had not yet read Montaigne, but I was already applying, without knowing it, one of his principles: "I don't think too much about how I'll get out of a dangerous situation, but about how little it matters that I do." Drafted to Morocco until the bases were evacuated one year later, for it was at the time of the war in Algeria, I shared the lonely existence of young recruits who had come over from France. One of them used to put on his civilian clothes once a week and, wearing a tie, look at himself in the mirror, then without a word dress in his uniform again.

Tuned in to the airwaves of radio Morocco, every evening I heard the Algerian national anthem sound out on the programme "Voice of Algeria". I found it very beautiful and I managed to teach it to the choir in my section. This was my only claim to fame during this war. I knew that the French presence in Algeria was unjustified. The only regret I ever had, until this day, was that I didn't have the courage to desert, out of solidarity with the Algerian people. Some did, like General de La Bollardière, who spoke out against torture and was placed under arrest in a fortress. Not I: at nineteen and a half years old, my political conscience was not yet sufficiently strong to take such a decision. I was still a long way from being free of the influence of my family.

After the evacuation of the French bases, I was transferred to France, where, for three months, I was assigned to training a section, composed of men from the Martinique and Alsace in equal share. I learnt a lot about men, getting people from totally different backgrounds or behaviour to live together day and night.

Then I was drafted to a tactical air base, where I had an office with a sign "National Defence Secret." In fact no-one was allowed to come in, regardless of rank. My work consisted in adding up the amount of fuel used by each section. This huge, ultra secret task took me one hour a month. I used the rest of my time to read a book a day. Which didn't stop me from crying for joy for the first time in my life, on the day I was finally freed, in the train that took me back to Paris.

A year later, I was goose stepping down the Champs Elysées dressed in a German uniform. I am neither proud nor ashamed of this since it was for Jean-Pierre Melville's film: *L'Armée des Ombres.* If there is a journalist who would like to quote just the first half of this sentence, I could be accused of saying just about anything. I was also a journalist in *Fantômas*, with Jean Marais. The Army, which doesn't like journalists, may not forgive me. I was also a Roman soldier in *La Passion du Christ*, then halberd bearer in *Chatterton*. It was while this last film was being made, that I caught a glimpse of myself in the studio toilets mirror, wearing a wig of bright orange hair, that I said to myself: "My dear Paul, stop making such a spectacle of yourself." Which is how I came to give up this student job.

Sometimes, on certain winter evenings, some past *cailíns* from days gone by came back to hover around the turf fire. The one that came back to taunt me that evening had already done so on the day we met, when she appeared wearing her mysterious halo. Her queenly carriage was that of a dancer. This is what she did at the *Opéra*, and it showed in the way she moved. We had taken a night train to go and fetch a motorbike in the depths of Switzerland. Alone in the compartment, I slept in your arms. A trace of the unsayable had installed itself in the shape of your old-fashioned underclothes, something which awoke old fantasies within me. Outside it was cold. Your heart reddened with warmth as you roared. My imagination wandered from station to station. I was filled with happiness at having found you. Filled with fear that I might lose you.

Then there was the Bernina pass on the motorbike, in the snow, your arms around my body. The coffee in Italy. A postcard which you didn't send. A coffee in Saint Moritz in the early hours of the morning.. Love's universe, simply love in that palace where we were the only occupants. Those empty corridors, full of scattered bins. Those silent rooms, no light, nobody. That vast, monumental staircase, too big for the two of us and yet which came to life under the sound of our footsteps, marked out by the rhythm of our arms, our hands, our interlaced fingers. At the break of day, under your white helmet, all the treasures of the world were reflected in your eyes, so much so that the bare beauty of the Alpine slopes paled by comparison.

The smell of turf brought me back to my own green hills, far from the Alpine highways. I kindled the fire, and seating myself again in the old armchair, the same *cailín* came to taunt me once more. To say to me: "Let me become your past." I hadn't wanted to do so. I found my past too heavy to carry. So I left it on the roadside and went on my way, my shoulders still sore from the straps. Yet invisible reins still tied me to it. I had as well say: let me move on, it would have none of it. If only it had let me go on. Then I remember answering *cailín*: "I love you too much to let you slip between my fingers." Then she disappeared once again in the wreathes of smoke which swirled around the tomes in my library.

Ah love! Shall we try to talk about it? You're on. Sit tight. Since time immemorial, throughout the world, literature has brought its own grain of wisdom to this teetering edifice. Since Sumer, from the love songs of ancient Egypt to Brassens "don't throw stones at the adulterous woman, for I am just behind her", without forgetting Lacan "Woman does not *ex-sist*", may I add my own pebble, my tiny pebble, my grain of knowledge, experiences, thoughts, certainties, uncertainties, beliefs for all this and more? I never shuddered in the morning as I passed in front of my caretaker's lodge, having spent the night rewriting the world of love anew.

First of all a fact: a large number of men on this planet are polygamous, whether it be in Africa, the Middle East or the Far East. It is a fact against which American feminists, in spite of their screaming, can do nothing. I'm not saying that it is either good or bad, it's just a fact. Full stop. The remaining men on this planet are also polygamous. Whether openly, like the Mormons, or secretly, like our own kings and their mistresses. Here is the advice given, over four thousand years ago, in a poem from ancient Egypt:

> Keep away from the woman outside
> Do not look at her as though she were superior to her own,
> Do not acquaint yourself with her body:
> She is like deep water,
> Whose hidden currents are unknown.

A woman whose husband is far away,
Tells you every day: "Look, I am lovely!"
When she has no witnesses.
But if she is found out, it is a fatal error.
Men will do much harm,
Thinking it will remain secret.

(Extract from *the Wisdom of Ani*)

On the other hand, Greek mythology, which is simply the projection of our desires, has accustomed us to all manner of deception and vengeance.

So, and now what is to be done about this reality and its contradiction: love is exclusive and at the same time there is always the underlying desire to look elsewhere. For oneself of course, but certainly not the other person! This problem has been partly resolved for man by the harem and its guardians, the eunuchs. However, a Nigerian man, Mohamed Bello, has just been sentenced for having 86 wives, whereas Islamic law, the *sharia*, only allows four. [33] It's more difficult for women. But they don't come off so badly given that one child in every five is not their husband's child. [34] Maupassant's wonderful short story: *L'Inutile Beauté (Useless Beauty)* is an eloquent exposition of this subject. Even the priests get round the problem; in Africa, they are obliged to make love to the nuns, they say, because African women have Aids. [35]

In Vietnam, to this very day, every Saturday evening there are big dances of about six hundred people where established couples can meet, then go their separate ways, find a partner for the night and then return to their conjugal homes the next morning. Don't all rush over; these dances are closed to foreigners!

So how does one get around all this? Pivotal love is one solution. As for me, I follow the precept of

Brassens: Don't throw a stone at the adulterous woman, for I am just behind her! How can I express my desire for the married woman? For me it's quite simple. First of all there's the attraction of that which is forbidden, even though the husband has to remain unknown to me, therefore he cannot be a friend. That's too easy. On the other hand, as the official role has already been allocated, I feel reassured. I do not need to engage for any length of time. Commitment, for me, is like waiting on death row. It doesn't suit me. I need to know that I can reverse. I want to be free to do what I think I can or should do.

Convinced of the certainty of my theory, I fell under the spell of a lovely Irish woman. She was married and lived in Belfast where she had a job. The two hundred kilometres which separated us, her social and marital situation, suited me perfectly. Her episodic visits kept our desire alive without sinking into a routine. Then one evening, coming home from the pub at two in the morning, there were twenty or so messages on my answering machine. Without ever having hinted at this eventuality, she told me: "I've left my husband and my job: I'm on my way to join you!" The last message stipulated "I'm sitting on my suitcase twenty kilometres from you, I'm waiting for you."

I, who thought I was safe because of her position! Men are not so rash. A woman's determination knows no bounds. Like the Parisian woman who wanted to leave her husband for me. I tried to dissuade her. I had as well point out the virtues of her husband, all to no avail. Out of desperation she told me that she was pregnant with my child. It took me a few weeks to realise that this was just a strategy – there never was any gestation – to get me to commit myself; which I obviously did not do. Her excuse was that she wanted a child bearing my name. I was obviously touched, but a child should not be a victim of a strategy. In general the feminist leagues preach the contrary: "It's us who do the work for nine months and it's the man's name which is given!" And of course! It's exactly because the woman did all the work that you have to register the father. For imagine that in addition to providing the physical conditions, the woman also supplied the symbolic element; what place would there be left for the father?

The insertion of the drop of sperm entails some form of registration. The father is the kingpin of creation. The mother is the Achilles' heel. Marilyn French, who despite her name, is an American feminist, claims in her *History of Women*, in over one thousand and eight hundred pages, that "to name children after the father is an intrinsic act of violence and overrules the natural right of the mother." Such absurd ideas certainly don't encourage you to read the rest! Yet it is not enough for the father to be sexually involved if he does not consciously accept his fatherhood. Without which, there can be no fatherhood. Even at that, it is not enough to symbolise the father for him to exist. How many times have I heard the sentence: "My son, it's very simple, his mother gives him everything." By saying this, the father confirms his non-existence! Themistocles recognised this himself because his son took advantage of the affection that his mother bestowed on him, leaving the father to confess that "My son has more power than any man in Greece, because the Athenians rule the whole of Greece, I rule the Athenians, it is she who rules me and he rules her." If the conqueror of Marathon and Salamis had not been present as a father, he ended his life as father of a nation by betraying his country and taking refuge with Artaxerxes, the king of the Persians whom he had driven out and in whose abode he took his own life.

In order to exist as a father, the child must at first be acknowledged in all senses of the word: what you have done, I acknowledge, therefore you exist. The loveliest smile that I ever saw: that of a two-year old child seeing the drawing he had given his father on his desk. One of the premises that allows the father to play his role is to manage to separate the woman he married from her own mother. If this relationship is too confining, it will be as difficult to win over as the womb of an old spinster, even though by definition I have no experience in this domain.

It works in the opposite direction too: in order to rebel against the father, he must at first exist. Talleyrand rebelled until he became the perfect class defector. To exist does not mean to overvalue. If you overvalue your son he will become the child king, always looking for the inaccessible crown. If you overvalue your daughter, you will turn her into a phallic woman, who will succeed socially, but that is all! Furthermore, she will satisfy herself with the privilege due to her self-assurance, which is the definition of racism: to accept a privilege because of one's race! In either case, they will pass over that which is truly essential: life itself!

My solitary life went on without problems. Only village events disturbed my peace from time to time. For eight days or so Tom, my farmer neighbour, had been missing. His dogs, which were starving, were running around the house. No-one was too worried. This fifty-year old bachelor sometimes escaped off to Dublin to see the girls. At least this is what some whispered with a knowing smile. Going down to the town I walked alongside the little stream of brown water, coloured by the bog that it crossed. Near the little stone bridge covered in ivy, I was stopped by Johnny who was standing near a shed in his shirt in the rain, saying to me:

- There's a bad smell coming from there, I daren't go in alone, will you come with me?

We both went in. Tom was there. His left hand was fixed rigidly at his neck where he had tried to undo the rope from which he had been hanging for several days. Suicides are not uncommon here, but this was the first that I had witnessed. The awful stench pursued me for some weeks, even though I was at some distance from the site of the drama. When I thought of Tom, the sight and smell followed me. Lost in my thoughts, I was pursued by a hanged man. Like lost loves who, years later, come back to haunt you. Once they stop moving, we think of them buried, under the ground, a huge cross stuck through the heart. But those buried souls do not always stay put.

I had thought of this possibility for myself on more than one occasion. Faced with the reality, I had said to myself: "Suicide interests me to such an extent that I would like to study it for a little longer." This is how I learnt that the suicide rate is highest of all amongst farm labourers. In fact, what had they to hope for in life? Having never begun to live as they'd wished, and finding their aspirations difficult to achieve, why should they fear ending their lives? Being so consciously well-disposed, such a step cannot seem so daunting…

Here, death is part of the life of the town. The wakes and burials are occasions when people meet, share jokes and have a drink. I understood here more than anywhere else that it is in accepting death that you learn to live. The humour and *joie de vivre* of the Irish are in direct proportion to their acceptance of death. They know too that, as in the expression for such an occasion, you never see a chest of gold follow a hearse. This is also what I tried to teach my young son, to put money in its place. Then, on one of my trips to Paris, we were having a drink on the terrace of a café near a set of traffic lights when a hearse stopped accordingly in front of us. A few minutes later, a security van for collecting money pulled up behind it. And my son cried out: "Dad, you're wrong, look!" Adolescents always know better than their fathers. And sometimes they are right. And this is how I answered him.

The village priest, with whom I maintained a cordial, albeit non-religious relationship, had just told me that he had discovered in the archives of the parish that in the XIIth century there had been a convent on the site of my cottage! I didn't doubt that this place had been blessed by God. I told him that this explained why on certain windy nights I sometimes heard and even saw a few ghostly, lovesick noviciates wandering around my cottage. As he took leave, he called out: "Paul, watch the nuns!"

- Don't worry, I said to him, the fantasy of deflowering a nun, even eight centuries too late, has never tempted me.

To say that I had never slept with a nun would be a lie. It was summer and my father had rented a drafty old castle in the centre of the Grande Chartreuse for the holidays. It was one of my first trips to France. Alone in a huge bedroom, in the middle of the night, I was awoken by a sort of regular hissing. Scared to death, I took refuge in the bedroom of my eighteen-year old cousin who was a noviciate, saying to her: "There's someone in my room, I'm too scared, can I sleep in your room?" I ended the night in her bed, far from the hooting owl which had terrified me; I was twelve years old. *Honni soit qui mal y pense*, even though behind every fear there is desire... The irony is that she is now the mother superior of the very orphanage where my father left me for one year.

During the day, the owner of this imposing castle took me into the dungeons, for more noble pastimes. He showed me all the plans he had drawn up for the invention of the water plane. I was fascinated. I like to think that it is thanks to him that I have learnt to surf through life.[36]

Perhaps the insistence on all that was sacred, drummed into me by my father since childhood, accounts for something in the absence of fantasies concerning nuns. In fact, every time we went to France, my father, who was very devout, worked out the stages of our journey in accordance with the holy sites. I will not list the numerous Spanish, Portuguese and French cathedrals, only those high places such as Fatima, Compostelle, Saint-Bertrand-de-Comminges, Lourdes, Notre-Dame-de-La Salette, Ars, Lisieux, and others I can't remember...

Tanked up with this successive impregnation at such an early age, like an overfed scallop, I clung to my faith like a limpet to a rock. Such impressions end up working their way through your insides until they leave their mark. Adolescence and the baker's daughter saved me from this sticky pass. But it took me a few more years to appreciate good bread without feeling guilty. The Africans say that: "The donkey never leaves good bread." Since I am a little African, and as stubborn as a mule, I put this notion into practice. If I don't receive good bread every day, the manna sometimes appears in the form of a *brioche*. In the same way that the best cake and bread bakeries are to be found near churches where good Catholic people indulge in a little sin after mass, it can be deduced that young girls raised in a Catholic environment, where the unleashing of emotion will be the greater for having been forbidden more than in most religions (the inaptitude of protestants is distressing), will prove themselves real artists whenever they let go.

If the bakeries situated around the little country churches are better, then those near the cathedrals are more refined: I knew the one at Reims very well, since it was there that I did my military service, and I can also testify to the one at Chartres, where I went to high school. As for the one in Paris, I gazed down at it for twenty years from my window, and I can say that it wasn't far from my conquests' quivering. In fact, I lived at that time on the quai d'Orléans in the same spot chosen by Proust as Swann's home, which earned the riposte from the narrator's mother: "So, Mr. Swann, you still live on the quai d'Orléans, near the warehouses? I suppose it's in order to be nearer to the station when you set off for Lyon?" And again: "She never could understand why Swann lived on the quai d'Orléans, which without ever daring to admit it to him, she found beneath his station." The Ile-Saint-Louis was not very sought after at the time, having been thought to be too close to the wine depot. I managed to sell this apartment before the Ile Saint-Louis became what it had always been: a place devoid of much interest, now mostly lived in by Americans. Life consisting of more than a mere apartment, I never had time to regret it, nor, as they say in the South-West with reference to this, "to have a mouth like a turkey's arse!"

Having exhausted the cathedrals, I had to find something else. There remained the basilicas. It was in the fine features of a real Mary, born in the shadow of the Basilica of Lourdes, that the most delicious and forbidden bread was to be tasted. I don't know if it was the influence of Saint Bernadette, but she never managed to get me to play the wooden trumpet, the one sounded for the retreat. Only the brass one gave the 'la'. It was always the first time when her dress touched me as she passed by, [37] to such an extent that I asked her if she had a friend who was a doctor who could prescribe an anti-Viagra for me. I could have asked that daughter of the pharmacist-pharmacy store holder but, thinking this wouldn't be her domain, I refrained.

Among those delicious brioches I have known, there have been those who pretended they had a religious upbringing in order to increase their chances of seducing the coveted Adonis! But be careful, for if I give the medal to those girls who have grown up in the shadow of the cross, this medal has not always been a holy one. It's more a matter of 'butter wouldn't melt in her mouth.' Just as every medal has its reverse side, she had her perverse little game. Well aware of this game, I only smiled. The sexual alibi will be all the more rampant in proportion to the extent to which it has been contained, but it will still remain an alibi. Like the young couple who arrived with four enormous suitcases. She was worried she wouldn't have everything she needed, she explained to me. They were on their honeymoon. She was a stunning brunette, very outgoing, and at breakfast she said to me:

- He married me simply in order to fuck me; that's all he's interested in.The suitcases would never make up for what was missing, however red they were, crying out for attention. There will always be something missing for a woman. A man who is satisfied by physical pleasure may spend his life trying to understand what it is that's missing for her. How can he understand, since she herself often does not know... and yet she knows that 'that thing' is not there.

One good definition of religion has been given by Albert Einstein: "The word god is for me nothing more than the expression and product of human weaknesses, the Bible a collection of honourable, but still primitive legends which are nevertheless pretty childish. No interpretation, no matter how subtle can (for me) change this." [38]

I respect all religions and those founded on faith, because it makes a lot of things easier: "It is God's will." With a weakness for the Koran, however, for it is extremely tolerant. Having lived in Morocco, I can testify to this, whatever the fanatics say. They are to be found in every faith, notably in all the followers of the numerous Reformed Churches of the United States, where the Dollar is graced with the famous slogan "In God we trust." It has to be said that this country, which is officially secular, still has a President who swears on the Bible. Yet the Constitution guarantees, in its first Amendment, the separation of Church from State. Camus said: "between justice and my mother, I would choose my mother." To paraphrase him, I would say that between a classic Muslim and a fundamentalist born again Christian, I would choose a Muslim. [39]

Montaigne again, gives us a few tempting anecdotes on the subject of religious services:
"There exists a nation which, to nullify the sexual urge of those who came to mass, *garses* and *garsons* for sexual pleasure were kept near the church and it was advised to use them before attending the service. If they entered with a less than chaste conscience, it was at least because they had had their fill." [40] As for priesthood, he made it sound quite attractive to me:

"In certain countries, the priest opens the way for the husband, on the wedding day, in order to alleviate the groom of any doubt or question as to whether or not his betrothed comes to him in her virginity or violated by another lover." [41]

Now let's hear the Irish writers add their poetic voice:

"The Irish Catholics, assured of their just cause, got together to make a nation out of their country. Once again, as though it were necessary to prove it, the practising Catholics are very like other human beings… at times far worse." [42]

And again:

"(…) for he was a genuine religious man and one of the few religious men that was not a worse bastard than ordinary people." [43]

I won't devote any more discussion to this subject. Since religion can only be realised by the symbolic element of the imagination, it would be without end. And from there to what I imagine the reality of that symbolism is, we would never get anywhere! But if God existed, have you considered his metaphysical problem? I leave religion to those who have no other sublimation to fill the emptiness of their lives. It has to be said that Christianity has struck hard: the mother of Christ is a virgin. It's the dream of all Corsican, Sicilian, Spanish and Irish people: "My mother is a saint, she doesn't fuck." Ah, the 'Mama' and the whore! They are indelibly inscribed in the heart of every little boy.

As for the Holy Trinity, it is just a remake on the triad of Greek mythology, and all mythologies, sects, religions and philosophical systems. They always come in threes: the Hours, the Fates, the Graces, the Erinyes, the Grey Women, Eris and her golden apple, the Gorgons, even the Muses were three before tripling, and even Cerberus had three heads. Only Islam refused the triad.

There are a thousand and one nights. Don Juan had mistresses numbering *mille e tre*. It is much easier to call the third element the Holy Spirit and to say that Mary was both Virgin and Saint and then everyone is happy. And it works! Well, almost…

On the other hand I am certain that religion is very dangerous - and I can prove it : this article appeared in The *Irish Times* [44]: '*Child standing in school porch when statue of Blessed Virgin fell on him*': "A young boy sustained severe injuries to the head, requiring life support, after a statue of the Blessed Virgin fell from its pedestal and landed on top of him where he was standing in the school porch. The twelve-year old boy, Joseph, was taken unconscious to the general hospital. "
Poor Joseph! Two thousand years later he is still being pursued by a vindictive Mary for having refused to honour her. This happened to me also and I strongly advise against it!

"When we want to truss them up, we're phallocrats,
When we want nothing of it, a would-be Socrates."
(Georges Brassens)

This will be the title of my next work: *The Virgin Mary strikes again!*

This is what befell that brave priest, Urbain Grandier, who, sensing danger, refused to be the confessor at a convent. The Mother Superior, Mother Jeanne of the Angels, (she did exist) took revenge by accusing this worthy priest of having sent the devil to rape her along with several of the other nuns. He was tortured and burned alive by the Inquisition!

This makes me think of a drawing which tells the story of a young English virgin who wanted a child without any sexual relationship. Under the title: "A pregnant

Virgin", we see God seated on a cloud declaring: "If she thinks I'm going to acknowledge the brat, I've already been had once that way..."

The Irish nurture a cult of the Virgin and her statue is to be found placed here and there by the wayside of many little roads. These statues occur a little less frequently, however, than the diverse small churches of various faiths which are to be found on American roads. There are fewer, too, than the small Greek Orthodox repositories on Greek roads. If statues of the Virgin are becoming a little less frequent, it is because the faith is wavering more and more here. This doesn't stop the Irish from making the sign of the cross every time they pass a church or graveyard. One of my friends told me that his girlfriend was very taken by this superstition. It happened that she loved to 'fondle' him as he drove. It's true that the bumpy Irish country roads facilitate the process. The lady in question, what is more, was called Mary, would cease her activity every time she spied a holy site, bless herself, and then resume where she had left off. Alas, this story is only second-hand, but the sins of the flesh so condemned by the church have finally been sanctified!

On the other hand, if '*turlute*' (I find the word much more attractive than '*fellatio*') was practised by citizens of the Roman Empire, it was strictly forbidden amongst the elite. The honour of the Empire was based on virility, and such a passive act was considered effeminate. According to Suetonius, it was Nero's orgies together with this practice that hastened the fall of the Roman Empire. It was an unthinkable outrage. Some claim that the recent misadventure of an American president, whose status has been shaken, will lead the way to the fall of the American Empire for the very same reasons. [45] But alas, cause and effect are not always the same. Thirty-three centuries have passed between this poem and the fall of the Egyptian empire:

"I enter the water to be at your side,
And for love of you, I emerge, holding a goldfish.
He is happy cradled in my fingers
I place him on my chest."

(*Song of the Waterside*)

One day it happened that among my guests I received the lawyer who had been sent to the White House by the Public Prosecutor in order to indict the President of abusing his power with regard to a trainee member of staff. This lawyer was strongly opposed to the President and told me that: "I had in my briefcase all the relevant papers, and before I went into his office I said to myself, this time, mate, you've had it. Half an hour later, I left the Oval Office, my tail between my legs, so to speak, having been turned in my tracks and fallen completely under his charm! " It must be recognised that the recipient of the presidential seed confirmed loud and clear that she had acted of her own volition. In so doing, she is in perfect accordance with what Freud wrote on this subject: "Women have no problem acting spontaneously with regard to this much-desired fantasy, an innocent fantasy linked to the maternal breast and which does not require much imagination to see how it might become its substitute." [46]

Some feminists have wanted to call our attention to the fact that in this instance, it is the man who is in their hands. The phallic God having finally been spurned and thanks to the magic of their fairy fingers, they become the goddess who reaps the beneficial effects. They have simply forgotten that on Procrustes' bed they are but a means, and it is not they who will reach fulfillment. The man is not seated on the back seat, he's driving. To little Mary's delight, it's the passenger seat that she's sitting in, and with or without the sign of the cross, she knows this only too well. She also knows that it's just a promising preliminary and not the act in itself, hence denying her femininity and her own pleasure. Do we really need to remind ourselves that, contrary to a man, the eroticism of a sexual relationship is not, for a woman, limited to her vagina; far from it. Associated with it are both psychological, emotional, fantasy and – let's say it – mystical elements which may come foremost and all of which go to make up her erotic potential. Take, once again, Saint Theresa and her evident mystical climax. And this is no metaphor.

Since we are on the subject, the wonderful Michel Simon always demanded that there were a prostitute at hand to "give him a blow job" before going on stage. One evening, the unavailability of a professional woman meant that it was the female theatre director who had to carry out the task, without which, he maintained, the show could not go on.

As for metaphors, the Irish excel. Sometimes at their own expense. Poets are often invited to read a poem or tell a story on the radio:

- I write every day, says one of them, I was a genius from ten o'clock until half past twelve. Afterwards, I would drink. I wrote one poem a month, but as I got older I got slower. I would come to the end of the month without having written my poem and this became a physical obsession. It's just that I'm going through the male menopause. It exists, you know.
- And how does it manifest itself? Asked the journalist.
- Well I can't seem to write many poems, not even one a month. When you're young, you've got a lot of reserve energy. The next thing is, you learn to control it. Finally, as you get older, you can still do it, only with less force!

Then the journalist asked him what he thought of a musician:

- Oh you know, he wanted to ride two horses at the same time, and that's not easy! He could have done better, but it wasn't in his nature to go over the top.

Irish radio is a joy. On another occasion the presenter wanted to play us a song, but he couldn't find the record.

- I'm looking for it, in the meantime, speak to yourselves!

Then he came back, having left a silence of at least a minute.

- I've found it, it was under a book. In fact I must tell you about this book… and for quarter of an hour, he went on about how wonderful this book was.

Another day, there was a young man trying to explain Christian guilt:

- It's a bad state of conscience with regard to an illegal approach to a moral problem.

The journalist: Er, that is to say?
The young man: Well, in fact, it's pre-post Vatican II.
The journalist: Er..Well… Could you give us an example?
The young man: For example, it's like when you sneak a bit of bacon from Friday's pea soup. You feel so wracked with guilt that you go to confession, to relieve yourself of the guilt. Then you start over again half an hour later. In fact it's my mother who cultivated this idea of being guilty. I grew up in the country where everyone went to mass. Since I've been in Dublin, she phones me every Sunday morning to see if I've been to mass:

- You should go, because I'm your mother and I'm telling you to go. It's not my soul, but yours and it's your responsibility to see that you don't burn in hell.
- From early childhood we know what guilt is because we've got a clear and ever-present picture of hell.

Guilt was also the demise of old Philomena: when she came out of mass, she wanted to buy two cakes. The baker said to her "I'm closing soon, I've got three left and I'll give you the third one free!" On Monday morning Philomena went back to the bakery with these words: "You know the cake that you gave me for free, well it wasn't so good - I had an upset stomach all night!"

Another marvel of Irish radio is the weather broadcast: the best in the world. It is invariably right. Every morning you can hear the weather for the day: "Today it will be dry between showers."

What is also true, is that the Angelus is sounded out over the radio, in spite of increasingly vociferous objections. I think they also do it on television, but I can't confirm this, not having had a television for a very long time. Nor internet, nor anything else. I have time for myself; I am like the Arabs who say: "You have watches, we have time."

The Irish have a similar relationship with time, for here, feelings, the weather, the wind are all more important than money and how to get around. The most difficult thing round here is not getting work done, but paying for it. A local builder had done some work for me with a digger over a ten day period. It took me eight months to pay the bill. Every time I phoned him to find out how much I owed him, back came the reply: "No rush."

On another occasion I took a French journalist to visit a young artisan who, using old Gaelic weaves in her hand-woven tweed, works in her cottage overlooking the Atlantic. The journalist asked her whether she would send orders to France.

- Certainly not, I can't be bothered with making up parcels and all that sort of thing…

I went to pay a call on Jim, who had a small hardware store, in search of a drill bit.

- What do you want it for? He asked me.
- To make holes in my wall to put up bookshelves.
- Well take it and bring it back when you've finished.
- Tell me, if you won't sell it to someone who needs it, then who will you sell it to?

I was obliged to really insist, in order to buy it.

The roads of Donegal having got the better of the suspension on my Citroën DS, and the sea air the better of it's bodywork, I found myself without a car. Word got around in the town. A few hours later, a friend came by and threw a bunch of keys on the table.

- I heard your car is finished. You can't survive without a car. Here's one. I've got two cars and I don't need this one, so you can have it, because you need it.

There was no discussion. I ended by muttering:

- I don't know how I can thank you.
- No, he said, life's too short for that.

He died two years later of a heart attack. He was forty-two years old.

In Geraldine's yard there was an old telephone chair lying around in bits. She gave it to me. I asked a carpenter friend if he could repair it for me, even though a third of the pieces were missing.

- I haven't got much time, and there's a lot of work there to make up the missing parts.
- I'm not in a hurry.

I was just happy enough that he had accepted to take on the job.

Three months later he brought back the chair, gilded in a dark, glossy varnish, to my house.

- What do I owe you for the work? It's wonderful.
- Nothing. I did it for you. Because you wanted to bring it back to life. Otherwise, I wouldn't have done it!

I was never able to pay him.

Sometimes, without asking, things come along of their own accord. Ryan said to me:

- Your gate is all rusted away.
- It doesn't matter. I never close it.
- Yes, it does. I've got an iron one which I never use, it's at the bottom of my garden and I don't need it. You could do with one, so it'll be yours.

He brought it up to me and installed it. I was never able to pay him for it.

As I was saying, time and money, they don't really count it. When you've arranged to go and see someone, it's better to wait two hours before you turn up. It's called "Irish time."

A journalist from Limerick to whom I had sent a press release, replied that he didn't have time to come and see me, but that if I was passing through Limerick, I should look him up and we could have a drink together. Only an Irish journalist could write such a letter!

Irish wisdom is legendary and well-defined by the following expression: "They stand around all day breastfeeding the shovel."

Conviviality, mutual help and human warmth are all inherent in the Irish soul. It is particularly evident when people are reunited at Dublin airport, for example, where cries of joy ring out; whereas in Belfast, the coolness of the Protestant population does not allow such effusive behaviour.

If I like and still live in this country after so many years, it is not so much the realisation of a dream, in the sense that my dream would be…No, it was in response to an injunction. A nocturnal injunction which occurred during an enigmatic dream: in the dream I had to go to Donegal, but I didn't know why, nor where it was situated. All I could see were the capital letters which stood out distinctly: D.O.N.E.G.A.L.

I woke up with these capital letters in my head without understanding what they meant. I tried turning the letters over in various languages, but all to no avail; there was no meaning to be had. It wasn't until two years later that friends coming home from holiday told me that they had had a wonderful time in Donegal! All the colour drained from my face and at last I inquired as to where Donegal might be?

- It's a county in the north of Ireland.

I was hardly any the wiser, since the name meant nothing to me. After lunch I hurried to a bookshop where I bought a map of Ireland. I finally found Donegal on the map and recalled that I had spent a weekend there ten years ago and that I had stayed on the beach, reading until eleven in the evening.

And this was how, a few years later, I loaded my books into a little van and took the road for Donegal. I am still here to this day.

One other reason which led me to settle in Ireland was the hunger strikes of Bobby Sands and his comrades which were to end in the deaths of ten of the prisoners. The only demonstration I have taken part in was one outside the British Embassy in Paris so that the Iron Lady might grant political status to the inmates of Long Kesh, all the more so since Bobby Sands had been elected as an MP. She would have none of it, in spite of the missive transmitted to her from Epictetus: "I know when I see a slave who thinks he has succeeded and who is consumed by pride." [47] I told myself that young people who are capable of doing this kind of thing and going to the bitter end have got something to teach me.

It seems that she is now losing her head a bit, just like her old friend the actor-President, who spent his days raking up dead leaves which CIA agents then spread out for him again in order to keep him occupied. It's a sorry end for these two stars of liberalism. But as Coluche said: it doesn't matter that they've lost their minds, but those that have found them are in a bad way.

Life in the town went on through marriages and burials. Old Ted had just died at the age of ninety-six. He had been found on a number of occasions lying comatose on the side of the road. First the priest was called to administer the last rights, then the doctor in order to certify the death.

- No, no, said the latter, it's just an alcoholic coma.

But on this occasion the last slug of whiskey proved to be fatal. Every time I met him he never failed to remind me that it was he who had replaced the thatch on my cottage with slates. It was in 1936 he told me, and it was the first in the area to be done. I went to his funeral to pay my respects. To my surprise the whole town was there. It was then that I understood that when there was a death in a home, it wasn't just the family who had lost a loved one, but the whole community.

On another occasion it was the first time that I had heard trousers flapping in the wind like the wind in sails that are being lowered. There were a lot of trousers around the coffin in this little town. The high round tower which looks down on the little church by the sea was not shaking, however. It had seen burials without number. Only this one had a particular importance: it was the local doctor, to whom the whole town had come to pay their last respects. His imperturbable good humour always provided the words to encourage his patients in the middle of the night on muddy laneways. This good humour showed in the crowd, since the Irish, at all the burials I have attended, understand how to put death in its proper place. At the beginning it almost used to shock me, but now I'm happy to share life with those that remain. In the pub!

Having been considered too young to attend my mother's funeral, I compensated for this hole in my life by going to the first funeral that came along, even if my presence was judged superfluous. When I told this story to an Irish friend he remembered it when he buried his wife. He very much wanted his grandson, who was still very young, to come and see his grandmother in her coffin. Chance had it that I was present at the exact moment when the young lad came to pay his respects. Through an unforeseen transference, I identified with this boy and a wave of emotion overcame me, decades late. I had helped prompt this gesture of homage and now I found myself the unwitting beneficiary. Since that time I no longer go to funerals where my presence is not expected.

Since we are on the subject, I am reminded of the woman who spent her life looking after her physically handicapped mother. The mother died when her daughter was sixty-five years old and the latter continued to look after her by going to her graveside every day! Even death failed to break the weighty bond. I do not make light of the matter since I suffer from the reverse problem. I have spent my life trying to sublimate the hole left by that lack. An ungrateful task if ever there was one, as I had only an unconscious memory of her, nevertheless indelibly inscribed in my ventriloquist's bones.

The inheritance of the maternal link cannot be erased. "She gradually became predominantly what others were not. She left in me the embryon of an ideal of delicacy impossible to find in anyone ever after," as Philip O' Connor wrote.[48] In 1967 this Irish writer met Panna Grady, an American heiress, at one of the numerous sumptuous parties which she held in London in her apartment overlooking Regents Park, where artists were in the habit of queuing up for cheques to keep them going. According to Andrew Barrow, their first meeting was both historic and disasterous [49], since, after an electrifying exchange when their eyes met, Philip decided to throw the entire entourage of poets and so on out on to the street, insulting them as he did so. She let him go ahead and became his sixth wife. Refusing to travel to the United States which he loathed, they left fifteen days later for the south of France where they settled and lived together (and where Panna still does) until his death thirty-one years later. His daughter told me that, twenty-one years after they moved, on being invited to the neighbouring château for a party held in honour of a Canadian writer, he repeated the scene, only in reverse order. He called out to his wife in an adjoining room, shouting: "Panna, get me out of this bloody place, get me away form these bloody bourgeois people. Get me out of here, now!"

Sixty years later the maternal inheritance was still wreaking its havoc.

It's for this reason that I am against inheritance. But the *crater* still persists, even if at times people feel it is no longer there. One had well adhere to the illusions and fantasies of another person, for they are but crutches and rarely up to job. The adherence will never be perfect. It's like trying to recreate the contours of a rock that a fault has caused to split apart. Even the greatest precision can never touch the original fusion. In the beginning there was the fault !

I sometimes blithely throw myself into this fault, thinking I might find a prop for my childhood impulses. But as soon as I recognise it as just this, it changes everything and I accept the slavery of tropism, for better or worse, no longer being taken in. Then I learn again to be what I am.

On the other hand, since absence is the best fuel for the imagination, I imagine and am still imagining. My imagination flows over the horizon and allows me to create the unimaginable. To create is to sublimate the void, an absence, a *crater*. Art is the expression of that void and not of a state of satiety. Debussy wrote *La Mer (The Sea)* in Burgundy. Joyce wrote *Ulysses* in Trieste. Blaise Cendrars never took the Transsiberian, "what counts is that I put you on that train", he said. Ravel composed *Habanera, la Rapsodie espagnole, le Boléro, Alborada del gracioso, Don quichotte a Dulcinée,* without ever having been to Spain. It wasn't until two years before his death that he finally visited the country.

The void, the absence, the *crater* cannot be filled by just anything. When it is filled with art, we all benefit. When it is filled by animals, we all have to suffer them.

I was going to the Haute Savoie with a young marquise who had recently divorced her marquis, foisted upon her by her father (she insisted on marrying in black, to show her scorn for her father's choice). We were trying to navigate as though in a drunken vessel, in her admirable 2CV, along minor French roads. My own company not being enough for her, she had brought her dog and her cat along on the journey. In spite of the very low fuel consumption of this wonderful car, we had to stop to fill up from time to time. Without my noticing, the cat made good use of one of these stops to escape through an open window. We each went in our separate directions in search of her. I finally spied her in a garden. I crept in as quietly as possible and dived on the animal. He fought back a bit, but I managed to keep hold of him, like a trophy, all the way back to the car. When I reached the vehicle all I heard was :

- How could you have mistaken that horrible animal for my darling pussy? - which, in the meantime, she had found.

Love had rendered me blind. In diving into the briars I had been unable to distinguish the true from the false. I know we must call a cat a cat, but it has to be the right one. The draught stoppers shaped like long sausages are the only cats that sit quietly at the bottom of my cottage doors and which have a useful purpose, since they prevent the bad old wind from coming in.

To be in love with an animal lover is to have a dog's life.

On another occasion, like two crazed magnets, I fell into the arms of an American woman approaching her forties. She paid me several passionate visits then invited me to New York. I had always refused to take a trip to this country, not wanting to suffer whatever was waiting for us here, in a near futur. Alas, passion may lead you to do things that even a madman would never have thought of. I fell straight into the trap. She was waiting for me at the airport in New York with her dog, which she had had blessed on the preceding Sunday in the local church where all the women had gone with their pampered pooches. "It was really cute," she told me. When we arrived at her charming Manhattan apartment, her dog began to show signs of a growling jealousy. So I asked her to put it in the next room so that we might link up again without any little snags: for there was no doubt about it the beast had taken a disliking to me. I had hoped for a romantic candlelit supper on the terrace. Seeing nothing which hinted at this possibility, I suggested we dine in town: "But no, we're in America here, I'll phone for a pizza." It was true; I had in fact forgotten that we were in America. No intimate, lovingly-prepared little dinners. After three days of pizza at any hour, as I surveyed the beast in the corner which vomited on the floor just to underline his ingratitude at my presence, we finally went out to look around the city, without forgetting the inevitable 'ground zero'. As we walked around Manhattan, I didn't see the beggar sitting on the ground next to his dog. She said to me: "Look, Paul, poor dog!"

The dimensions of the *crater* can lead us into some sinister places. She, who hated her father, was comforted by the downfall of this man whose decline had fuelled his love of animals. I established that her friends and neighbours in the little block where she lived were also just like her: of varying ages, nearly all of them single, but attached to dogs or cats which filled their every conversation. So I decided I would prefer to take the first plane back to Dublin.

"Seeing some foreigners, rich and opulent men who were all carrying little dogs and monkeys, doting on them hopelessly, Ceasar asked whether the women in their country didn't have children: thereby wisely rebuking those who show a tendency to love, to give affection and charity that nature gave us to express in our relationships with men and not animals." [50] Coluche put it in a more amusing way: "There are people who have children because they can't afford to buy themselves a dog."

The only dogs I esteem are those who have taken their name. [51] I am of course talking about the Cynics: Antisthenes, Diogenes, Crates, Bion and all their disciples who, through their asceticism, wanted to prove their scorn for all wealth, moral and social conventions. "If you are able to do without wealth, then you have something more important and worth far more than wealth itself." [52]
I won't mention Cerberus since it is he who would have the last word!

The Australians found an idea to fill their void. On the western side of Australia rain is infrequent and the rivers are therefore often dry. To fill the void of Protestant Sundays, the authorities of a little town organise bottomless boat races in the river. Each boat is manned by ten runners and they engage in a frantic race in spite of the heat. But from time to time the void fills up in an unforeseen manner: a big storm fills the river with water. The town crier has to run about the streets announcing: the boat race has been cancelled because there's water in the river.

The void, the absence, the *crater*, one had as well sidestep; it has to be overcome, if one is not to be sucked under. The writer and journalist, Lucien Bodard, was considered one of the greatest reporters of the Indochina war. He spent his days at the hotel, sipping whiskey, waiting for the return of his fellow journalists who had gone off to the scene of action. When they came back, he listened to the stories of what they had seen, and then he wrote his own report. Being absent from the battlefield, his imagination was fuelled by the first-hand accounts which he heard, and which lent unequalled strength to his articles. The absence of reality was thus sublimated, thanks to his art.

When neither art nor culture are present, what is there left for the poor soul, wounded in childhood, to fill his *crater*, if not perversity or betrayal; for in choosing this mode of expression, the wounded soul will have the impression he exists. Evidently this is not the case. It will cling for a while to the illusion, then fall down once again, at times a little further down. It so happened that I was once identified as the ideal man. I had as well tell her that I would never be this Mr Right to whom she aspired, but that I was just the prop for an emotional charge which arose from her childhood, and that the reality of who I was didn't count for much within that, all my reasoned explanations carried no weight faced with her irrational impulses. I had become the mooring post for her imagination. The only solution therefore was show myself in all my blunt reality. Sometimes, though rarely, I managed to make sure that the idealisation was not total. At which point everything became possible. In the opposite case, all relationships were impossible.

More than once in my life I was caught up in the idealisation that is the lot of a person who receives love letters. In this case love might express itself asexually by firing all the other attributable values, whether real, supposed or imaginary. This is where the trap is, because she will always end up believing that these same values are ineluctable, whereas they only last as long as roses, whatever the sexual force which may occur as a result. The love letter is the sexual sublimation of the staircase: the expected desire as one ascends will always fall short of that which is experienced, and we are lucky when the senses are not turned upside down.

To use another metaphor, I could talk of a veil: that of the nun when she enters her vocation, that of the bride and that of the erotomaniac when used as part of her lure. Whatever the case "it" always takes place elsewhere. I need all three: the symbolic letter, the real staircase and the imaginary veil which encompass all of these. It is at this point that everything becomes possible if I accept these props for this make-believe.

Just as the unenclosed cell loses all its honey and thus its essence, dear ladies, do not turn your noses up at being enclosed, otherwise pornography will win the day. There is nothing sadder or more sexually off-putting than nudity which is thrust in your face. I am speaking from experience. Just like the young woman who, also speaking from experience, undressed and opened her legs when faced with being raped. The rapist fled helter-skelter. I have read several studies recommending this solution. I can see that this may not be easy for a young woman who has been attacked. It is nevertheless true that if the forbidden element of an act of violent transgression no longer exists, then the rapist no longer has a motive.

The existence of the veil is a condition of desire. This is what American women have never understood. It is true that their Anglo-Saxon inheritance is partly to blame. As for the Irish, I think that the influence of the British over six centuries must have something to do with the difficulty they have in using a veil of seduction. The very veil that the feminists have thrown in the nettles, or rather burnt in public places, as being an affront to their identity as women, and which has only ever been used to titillate the desire of men and their unworthy wish to reduce women to the status of an object.

This is what one of the successive American chiefs (chieftaines?) of American feminists thought, until...

until… At sixty-one years of age, she fell in love and married. She was immediately repudiated by her stalwarts of former times. I can just imagine her wandering around her New-York apartment in frilly knickers and uplift bra. After so many years of denial and frustration, she must have become a fiery expert. I must tell you that one of the first inventors of the modern bra in the 19th century, was called *Caresse*!

American feminists have a limited knowledge of history. This shouldn't be held against them, for it would seem that this subject, like geography, isn't really taught in the United States. Most citizens whom we meet here demonstrate an almost baffling ignorance in these two subjects. They ought to know that until the Renaissance, young women bathed naked in the Seine. Protestantism changed all that, up until the 19th century. From the ankle up to the neck, nothing was to be seen. Sometimes an ankle was glimpsed, and all manner of fantasies set in motion: "When you see the ankle, the leg tends to suggest itself." [53]

I went to a session of Flamenco song and dance with a *cailín* in a little village in Andalusia. Only the men who standing around the stage admired the sight of the long dresses as they swirled under the moonlight, occasionally affording the glimpse of an ankle which provoked fanatical *Olés*. They were standing on tiptoe to get a better view of the object of all their fantasies. Then they sat down again to await the next dance. It was then that I recognized one of the earlier dancers who had come out from behind the stage in order to sit with the audience. She was dressed in ordinary clothes, that is to say without her long dress which had been replaced by a mini skirt. She threaded her way through the rows of seats without drawing any attention to herself. When you reveal everything like that, there's no place left for desire, said Coco Chanel of the Courrèges mini skirt.

On another occasion, a long time ago, I was walking hand in hand with a *cailín* by the water's edge on a beach not far from Casablanca. A couple of Moroccans were walking ahead of us: only the piercing eyes of the woman were visible beneath her black veil. She lifted the hem of her *djellaba* to her knees in order to keep the garment out of the spray from the little breakers. With the help of a few more lively waves, she raised the garment to her waist, revealing an adorable pair of knickers. She continued to stroll along the beach in this manner, completely unabashed, since her face remained hidden. A veil has something both good and beautiful! Without the veil, I wouldn't have remembered the incident today. A veil, whether it hides one's buttocks or one's face, has a purpose and when it conceals both at once, my ventriloquist's eye is shaken from its slumbers. More than once on the streets of Casablanca, or on the dusty tracks of the outlying valleys of Atlas, I crossed the path of female silhouettes, whose ember-black eyes were the only thing one perceived as they shot bewitching poison-glances at us. As my senses lay disarmed, at that moment I wasn't thinking about feeling the body which I knew to be naked under those numerous garments. What was exposed, because of the veil, was her ventriloquist's eye. Behind that veil there was meaning. And senses, too.

What made less sense was when the Whites went to Africa to dress the Blacks. Nudity is an offence to God, they said. Now they go there to set up nudist camps: and it's our sense of the erotic which is offended.

As you may have noticed, I am quite interested in the relationship between men and women. Wanting to better inform myself on this subject, I found myself a work devoted to the subject. It was written by an ethnologist, an honorary member of the *Collège de France*, who pulled off a great tour de force, in spite of his two volumes, of never mentioning the subject of male erection. I am using the medical term on purpose, since it fits better with this kind of learned work. The author does, on the other hand, confirm that matriarchy has never existed… it was simply a myth. So we're very much reassured. Stamping out erection is, however, the best way to achieve equality between the sexes. Fortunately or unfortunately, it does exist. It is even at the most primal root of male-female relations: Can I seduce him, she says to herself; will I make it, he says.

Having got round this first obstacle, which isn't always the case, I have on occasion balked at the first attempt. In spite of her charm, her pleasing body, nothing would work. I took this non-event upon myself, citing tiredness, worries, that I was coming out of a difficult break-up; in fact almost anything so that she wouldn't feel that it was her sex-appeal that was the problem.

The energy with which I presented my excuses made her doubt their truth. There was one woman, who, feeling her femininity to have been denied, headed for the door in fury. I was angry with myself, not because of the fiasco, but for having allowed myself to be led into a situation where my real interest was relatively limited. If she fails to awaken the unspoken core in me, it's very unlikely to work. There's a type of overwhelming beauty which can have the same effect: there is no room for the imagination, which underlies all desire. If she is the epitome of beauty, how can desire take over? It is not just two bodies which come together, but two subconscious minds which follow, or rather lead or at least their symptoms do. As was the case with the *cailín* whose father was an RAF pilot who died when he crashed his plane before she was three years old.

Then the illusion is no longer parked on a garage forecourt, but running on the stream of a mirage. This illusion allows time to halt its flight, and the substitute for the subconscious can dictate its law, for the better. Then time comes back to stake its claim. With its retinue of habits and routine, desire fades away. There exist a few guiles to make it live on a little longer. Then it collapses again, splattered like a cow pat. Changing pastures is one way out. There are others, such as pivotal love. Brassens tells us:

> "Ninety-five times out of a hundred,
> A woman gets bored making love.
> Whether she tells or confesses
> It's not every day that you brighten up her bottom."

He goes on:

> "Except when she loves a man tenderly,
> She gets bored without noticing."

Then:

> "The "more", the "that's it", the "go on"s
> Are just so that her partner
> Believes himself to be a great lover,
> So that the foolish and pretentious cockerel
> perched up high
> Won't be disappointed."

I can confirm, should I need to, the assertions of this great connoisseur. In order to make the illusion last a little longer, avoid over-decorated ceilings. Avoid animal-lovers, those that stroke their cat or dog, to assuage the jealousy of poor pussy or fido, just to reassure them that the lover who's humping away up there is only passing through. This intruder will join the ranks of the other lovers who have disappointed her: those who only think of screwing. Whereas you, my darling little dog or cat, or sometimes both, you will always love me and I will always be there for you. I have been party to this unpleasant arrangement. One I've never known is the woman who fell asleep while he was hard at it. My source is trustworthy, but I decline on any account to give it away.

This state of affairs confirms the poor quality of sexual encounters of most women, apparently liberated, in the full flush of their forties, having had husbands, children, and a sufficient number of lovers to give you that impression. Take, for example, the forty-five year old American woman who didn't know the difference between a circumcised or uncircumcised man.

If, on occasion, I have encountered those experts who are among the remaining five per cent, the party didn't last long. They quickly joined the other ninety-five. Brassens was well within his estimation. A man experiences sexual pleasure through a body: his own. He doesn't reach a climax through the woman's body; he only does so through his own organ. Whereas a woman's sexual pleasure is not felt through her body, she experiences it through what the man represents for her. And this man, however much she admires him, and in spite of his sexual prowess, which may be appreciated, will never be enough.

Only promises might bridge the gap. And those promises will always be dubious for her. There will always be a niggling little doubt. This doubt, which will remain outside his understanding, and the poor fellow will never get it: "What is it she wants?" he'll say. But it lies beyond her understanding of herself too; even she doesn't know what she wants, but she knows she feels something is lacking, and she knows this is not "it". This sexual pleasure a man can never know nor understand. He is forever destined to be the cuckold of the story!

For this need will never be modified. Just like the alcoholic: a thousand glasses will not be enough. Dionedes' barrel will never be completely filled. It is always someone else that one loves through the one who is there.

Just as alcoholism is not a problem of alcohol, sexual desire is not a problem of sex. It is when one's imagination has deserted one and there is nothing left to sustain the make-believe, that boredom creeps in. Only mystical ecstasy can be complete. There's nothing missing. Divine abstraction cannot disappoint. When you believe in it…

Between erection, which is the man's premise, and that sexual pleasure which "reaches beyond" and which is the premise of the woman, the equality of the sexes doesn't have a chance of seeing the light of day. What does see the light of day is the life which the woman gives to a child. By the miracle of gestation, a woman can experience the first quickening of the beginnings of creation. All men have spent nine months in their mother's womb. No woman has spent nine months in her father's belly. Something obvious which hardly needs to be mentioned: the relationship between mother and son, father and daughter, are not the same. One is visceral, the other symbolic. The equality of the sexes is such an obvious myth that we shouldn't need to be reminded of it.

One should not forget that a woman's life expectancy is about ten years longer than that of a man's, and that she can procreate until the menopause, whereas a man can do so indefinitely. The American feminists would say that this is unfair, but there is an even greater unfairness: since turning sixty I've never had as much success with women between thirty and forty years of age. If a woman in full bloom wins the first round, a man who wears his experience well, be it more or less proven, wins the second. As for the third, I'll talk to you about this one when she and I are in the old people's home. That's what we call life's injustice. In spite of which real beauty, whatever the age, is something which shows when you feel perfectly at ease with yourself.

If the collector accepted that he will never possess everything, he would be cured of his destructive passion and could begin to really live. In the same way, a woman might accept that she will never have all she hoped and longed for, if she accepted that "*between everything and nothing, there is almost everything, and that's not nothing,*" as Lacan wrote so well. She might then, in accepting this lack, finally reach sexual fulfillment in what is left over. It's with this "*it is not nothing*" that men and women are able to live together, and wonderfully well, as could be seen by the dinner of those eighty-year olds in the restaurant which overlooks Donegal bay.

I have spoken to you about love letters and have forgotten to speak about their corollary: the letter written to end a relationship. As I have one very good example, I give it to you here, unabridged :

'My dear Paul,

I won't see you on Thursday evening. I think it's much better that way. In any case, I'm getting married in eight days time, so it's all a bit ridiculous. I know I should have spoken to you about it on the phone, but I confess that I didn't think of it. It was only later that I realised. I hope you will keep as good a memory of me as I of you. N.'

No comment.

I am often thought of as being a lucky man. This isn't really the case. Luck is an attitude towards something we want accompanied by perseverance. Among the many student jobs I had, I used to drive an old woman three afternoons a week. Sometimes I took one of her friends back to the Quai d'Orléans, on the Ile Saint-Louis. I asked if she didn't have a small flat to rent. Yes, she said to me, I have a couple of young students who are leaving because they're getting married. I phoned her every two months to ask what was happening:

"They are married, they're leaving soon."

"She's pregnant, they're leaving soon."

"They've had a child, they're leaving soon."

After four years I finally got the apartment. Then she told me that she had just lost in a court case where the owner had taken her to court for sub-letting. I became the tenant by rights. Then, two years later, I bought it. It wasn't luck; it was four years of perseverance.

Wanting to create a book shop for books on music, I at last found a lovely premises full of charm. The place was always closed. I phoned every half hour. After ten days with no result, a voice replied: "You're extremely lucky, I was just passing to pick up my post." He was an architect and musician who wanted to get rid of his little workshop. Our business was quickly concluded. This is what luck is. But I'm not telling you anything new.

In order to set up a 'bookshop of books', as a neighbour told me one day, you need books. I looked at the catalogues of the two thousand publishers in France, in order to locate all the books which were in some way connected with music. A very learned publisher came at me one day with the following: "You're opening a book shop with just books about music, what are you thinking of. I've only got two books about music. That won't be enough to open a book shop." "You know, there are two thousand publishers in France, if every one has two books, that makes four thousand volumes. That's enough to start with." He had to acknowledge I was right!

Before this, a friend from Lyon phoned me to let me know that a neighbour of his was selling thousands of opera records at the flea market. Knowing I was a great fan of opera, he thought there might be some rare finds in amongst them. I went to Lyon. We went to his father's house, the latter having just died at eighty-five years of age, after spending his life buying all the opera recordings he could lay his hands on. There were thousands of them, including boxed sets that had never been opened.

"Dear man, I said, I don't want to buy any records because I'm worried I'll end up like your father, with unopened boxes." A collector buys all the records in order to have them, not in order to listen to them. We went out to have a convivial lunch together and I went back to Paris.

Six months later, when I decided to open my book shop, I phoned him to see if he still had the records and books, of which there were as many.

"Yes," he said, "I've changed jobs, and I haven't had time to do anything about them."

"Great, I'm on my way."

After a quick look through the books as a book shop owner, and not as a fan of opera, I bought the whole lot. The all-consuming passion of the father had turned into a burden for the son, whose own bedroom was stuffed full of records, even under the bed. If sleeping on *La Tosca* isn't that common, for him it was the beginning of his hatred of opera. I took the whole lot back to Paris in a lorry, including every publication on music to have appeared in the last fifty years. What had been a burden to the son became the joy of many music lovers like Vladimir Janélévitch [54] and Alain Resnais [55] who attributed me with being a walking miracle for finding him a book he had been unable to find for twenty years. I had become a miracle-maker for having gone to Lyon to get a lorry-load of books! The only real luck I had had, was knowing how to drive a lorry. I still remember coming back that night along the motorway with my *cailín* of the time sleeping, lying exhausted on top of a few tons of out of print books. That's what luck is. Not meeting well-known people, but ordinary, wonderful people who changed the course of my life. François Reichenbach had invited me to the private viewing of his film on Arthur Rubinstein, just before it was released. Seated between these two figures, the latter kept saying to me every two minutes: "fabulous, fabulous," referring to himself. The famous are always in need of reassurance!

I had met a lot of famous people when I was a student, since I used to drive an old English taxi cab to take customers from a well-known establishment favoured by night-time revellers, back to their homes. Several publishers asked me to give away some of the secrets that I had picked up on this crowd. Since betrayal has never been my thing, I always declined. Today, with the passing of time, I can give away a few anecdotes which are more cause to smile than be indiscreet.

The President at the time was Charles de Gaulle. His grandson, who bore the same name, and who was fairly inebriated, was going to have a last drink with friends. Then, when he was very drunk, he disappeared. His friends looked for him in vain. One of them became worried:

- He'll get stopped by the police. They'll ask him his name. When he tells them he's Charles de Gaulle, they'll take him straight to the nut-house.

Onassis and la Callas were regular habitués. There was a little room reserved for the sale of some quite amusing gadgets. That evening, Roger, who was in charge of the shop came and told me:

- I could write in my receipt book:

Onassis: Three francs !

In May 68 Jack Paoli was in a difficult position : he had just been awarded the *Légion d'honneur*:

- The students are going to think it's a thank you from the government for having handled the student confrontations as well as I could in my live report on the Gay Lussac street. Which was exactly what happened and he was mocked for his *Légion d'honneur*.

Under pressure from the demonstrators, the Prime Minister decided to free the four students who had been placed under arrest when the Sorbonne was under occupation (a good example, by the way, of the separation of powers...) In the evening their lawyers and a few journalists came to dinner to celebrate their liberation. Seeing that they were thirteen around the table, they asked me to join them as the fourteenth person. In a few hours I went from one world to another.

An American journalist asked me why we didn't sing the *Marseillaise* during the demonstrations. Obviously he didn't understand! In order to add to the fun, I played at being the snobbish golfer with my friends on the staff. I sent the wine back, saying it was corked, then the filet, saying it was over-done. They had the sense to play the game, coming back with such things as "Certainly, Sir." Then they added in a low voice: "Poncy golfer" (not knowing that it was a tautology.)

Still in May 68, the husband of a princess, turning up in his Porsche and a sky-blue shirt, declared between two glasses of champagne:

- But what on earth do these young people want? Everything's fine, life is wonderful in Paris.

Even then, I didn't have a television, by choice. A well-to-do man said to me :

- If they ask for me, say I'll be there in half an hour.
- Of course, I replied, what name shall I give?

He thought I was making fun of him.

- Guy Lux, can't you see.

Eugène Ionesco, whom I liked to meet in Montparnasse from time to time for a chat and an aperitif, said to me one day:

- In Montparnasse people recognize me and greet me in the street. In Saint-Germain, a little. On the right bank, never.

No comment.

Brigitte Bardot, with her sunburst beauty and dippy-drippy behaviour which was so sexually uninspiring, had announced what she was going to do with her life. I didn't have to wait until *the end of the day* to work it out. My friends made fun of me saying that it's because she was out of my league. I don't think so. What was on show was already close enough to put me off.

Alain Robbe-Grillet wanted to push me into his ravishing wife's arms, at all costs. She found me charming, he said. Knowing his taste and his books, I declined.

- Perhaps she's had a little too much to drink, I said. When we arrived at their house, he came back again with the same thing.
- It must be because she's only seen me from behind, was my saving quip.

Albert Vidalie, who was a poet and novelist, wore his heart on his sleeve. He insisted on my reading his manuscripts. I felt both honoured and confused. How could the young man that I was, give advice to a well-known writer, some of whose novels had been adapted for the screen, such as the *'Bijoutiers du clair de lune'* (The Moonlit Jewellers). But that is how it was. One evening when I was taking him home, we stopped as we often did, to have a drink in a café on the Place Denfert, opposite the statue of the Lion de Belfort. When the owner wanted to close, putting the last drunkards outside Vidalie said in his low, warm voice:

- You're joking, I can't go out. There's a lion outside that's going to devour me!

In his poem, *Les Loups* (The Wolves), sung by Serge Reggiani, he gets his revenge:

"Look now, you people in Denfert, look at him,
Under his green and bronze coat, the lion… is trembling."

In that establishment, which was frequented by a great many ham actors and pretentious journalists, I did meet a few exceptional people: The first will always be Albert Vidalie, then Jean Castel, since it is he, a generous and tolerant man, who proffered a glass of something or other at the drop of a hat, with a warm "let's drink to that". I never heard him put someone down. It's rare in those circles. Then there was Bernard Frank and Françoise Sagan who, however many drinks they consumed, never said a stupid thing. That too is rare. And Jack Paoli and his refreshing modesty. Sydney Chaplin and his crazy projects, which rarely came to anything, but he always greeted them with a big Zorba burst of laughter. Always in love, but never with the same woman, I had to act as alibi on a number of occasions in order to save his skin. Perhaps out of admiration for his father, I did everything he asked.

Finally, even at that time, there was an Irishman who was an English teacher in a neighbouring school, drunk one evening out of two, always grinning away under his mop of unruly hair, his tie askew, his trousers in disarray, very little money, but enough humour to render a whole regiment of Zouaves impotent. In writing these lines I realize that it was perhaps he who introduced me to Irish humour. These few people honoured me with their friendship, though they form but a short list, which unfortunately is exhaustive. The others taught me a lot about human nature… except that of the lawyers and company directors, dressed in three-piece suits, since they were banned from the premises.

The other evening I was admiring the view over Donegal and the little islands that fill the bay from my cottage on the hill in the company of an American, who said to me:

- You ought to build twenty little cottages with a swimming pool in the middle, you'd make a fortune.
- I'm too old to make a fortune, I said out of politeness.
- You're never too old to make a fortune, he went on, not wanting to give up.

He didn't know that I was just happy to have enough for my needs which weren't so very great. However many zeros you add to the dollar, it'll never change very much. If people want to satisfy needs which aren't really necessary ones, I'll leave that to those who have nothing else to do but that. Spending one's life working to achieve just that is the prerogative of those who have nothing better to do. This is what is so boring about Americans, that even in a truly idyllic setting, they can only think of money !

When I told this story to some Americans who seemed more open-minded, the man replied:

- Yes, I understand what you mean, but we're not like that. Then he got out a cricket set and started to play on the lawn.

After a few minutes, she said to me:

- Do you know how much we paid for that set? It was a real find…

I remained speechless, unable even to mutter an acknowledgement.

I think it's congenital. They have all been raised on the promise that they can aspire to all the riches in the world. That part which isn't already under their might, they suck dry. The only thing that counts is the result. They are very functional people. For example, they never appreciate the charm of the little lane spangled with fuchsia which leads up to my cottage. One of them was concerned that the grass which grows in the middle of the lane would damage the bottom of his car. Faced with such ignorance, I replied that it was his car that would more likely damage my grass. Another wanted a two-lane highroad. I replied that the day there was a motorway leading into the town, I would leave Donegal. And that's what I'm like; I can't stop myself from bringing their attention to the fact that the Americans want to rule the world and yet they are afraid of a small country road.

In their defence, perhaps they thought that my cottage was the epitome of the American dream. That which the puritan New-England founding fathers imagined they might erect: the house on the hill, a foreshadowing of the new Jerusalem and the kingdom of God on earth. The exemplary city which would enlighten the world.

In short, the chosen nation which will save the world. This is what the President declared as he led the country to war against Iraq: "God told me to go there." For do not forget that religion is deeply engrained in social, and hence, political life. Religion and pragmatism are happy bedfellows. Between the presidential "It was God who told me to," and "How much will it make us?" the vice president is making a profit somewhere.

The 1776 Declaration of Independence stipulates: "men have a right to life, freedom and the search for happiness." How Jefferson got thirteen rebellious colonies to sign such a thing is a mystery. Evidently, that mystery still works. The Americans still believe in it. They have a right to happiness. Moreover, according to them, achieving it is just a matter of money. To get this money they kill themselves working, quite literally! This is how a succession of widows, I mean women who have been widows of two or three husbands who died at the helm, have found themselves presiding over two thirds of the wealth of the United States.

Cynicism and naivety go hand in hand with religion. In the same way that Muslim fundamentalists in Arab countries have done, it is the fundamentalist Churches who have taken upon themselves the social and medical needs of those more needy people. There are forty-five million in the United States and, as in all the Arab countries, it works.

They won't be happy if I say that they use the same methods as the Muslim fundamentalists. However, not only do they use the same methods, but they go to South America and Africa to compete with them. I met both parties in the high valleys of Atlas… This mixture of populist nationalism, solidarity, democratic Messianism, religious moralising, radical conservatism will result in a national symbolism, incarnated by the stars and stripes banner, which encompasses all the ethnic minorities beneath the one flag of which they are so proud, that they display it at every opportunity, even on their jacket lapels, something which is unimaginable elsewhere. The flag has come to represent both a civil religion and a civic nationalism. All opposition is immediately considered as an act of anti-Americanism, a betrayal, an enemy of God and therefore of America itself. These values cannot and should not be questioned, otherwise the whole system would collapse. Freedom of thought is guaranteed, unless you decide to use it! Alexis de Tocqueville had already warned us about this in the 19th century: "I know of no country where there is so little real independence of spirit and freedom of expression as in America." [56] Or, again: "All the homegrown American controversies seem quite incomprehensible and childish to a foreigner." [57] Alas, since these values are shared by the two main parties, there's little scope for evolution. As under the Roman Empire, those who do not share the same values are considered "Barbarians", in the Latin sense of the word.

Black Americans who accept these values are well rewarded. As is often the case with class defectors, they only add to the cause. Like the grocer's daughter who became the English prime minister, the black American Secretaries of State have all played the democratic game they worked for very well. One of them by trying to prove the existence of arms of mass destruction, the other by justifying torture, all in the name of democracy…

Whatever the ethnic groups which make up the American nation, when they adhere to the founding credo of American civism, their ideological fervour makes 'real' Americans of them. I meet them here. Irish people, born in Ireland, who, after a few decades on the other side of the Atlantic, return with the American flag in their buttonhole. This can create some tension with those who stayed behind. Their way of thinking and their values have changed. Take, for example, an Irish friend who fell in love with an American woman. He invited her to Ireland. He quickly saw that "it wasn't going to work." Having done well on the back of the Celtic Tiger, he took her to Dublin and bought her a first class ticket back to New York. The Irish are like that, very generous. Touched by his generosity, she thanked him warmly:

- It was very sweet of you to get me a first class seat, she said.
- Don't thank me. If I could have hired a private jet to see you off sooner, then I would have done it.

I found the best definition of Americans in a book by Geoff Hill: "At the end of each day of making money out of thin air, of speculation without investment, of cleverness without intelligence and knowledge without wisdom, they drive home in their limousines. (…) It is not a pretty sight, to see people devoting all their energies to creating nothing other than wealth for themselves. And the worst sort of wealth: for rather than the vast, deep riches of love and laughter, food and art, this sort is only as deep as a dollar bill." [58] It's also worth reading the two following pages where Irish humour gives an hilarious insight into the American way of life.

American cultural media will talk about the success of a film in terms of the number of dollars it makes, whereas the French will refer to the number of people who went to see the film.

An Irish singer on tour in the United States was astonished that the Americans admired the Irish for their capacity to simply be themselves. I don't know if the lady who nearly had a private jet to go home in would have appreciated this. It is true that this is a very Irish quality. There is even a political party whose name is *Sinn Fein*, which means: We ourselves, or we by ourselves.

Even journalists are not afraid to put this principle into practice: at the time when America was preparing to bombard Iraq, the *Irish Times* [59] bore a huge colour photo of the American flag on its first page with the inscription: *God Bless America* with the 'B' crossed out, hence: *God Less America*.

The English were not lacking in response either: The *Guardian* [60] presented a drawing of the American flag where the stripes were shown as the bars of a prison behind which an orange detainee of Guantanamo could be seen languishing.

One of my guests was the *only* American diplomat to have resigned from his post to demonstrate his opposition to the war in Iraq. But I have also received supporters of this war. And that was more difficult. Two American women of this ilk, to whose attention I drew the fact that their President had killed more Iraquis than Saddam Hussein and more Americans than Ben Laden, remained unshaken. When they went out into the garden after breakfast and saw some rabbits hopping around near the house, they asked me if I had names for them. Without thinking, I replied: "Yes, that's Saddam Hussein and the other one over there, that's Ben Laden." They promptly made off, looking very offended. The names stuck and when clients phoned me in order to reserve a room, they often asked me for news of Ben laden. I would then imagine CIA agents listening in on my conversations, leaping up and down in triumph: "We've got him, we know where Ben Laden is!"

On the other hand, my two clients, outraged by my point of view, and faced with an undeniable fact, used a well-known feminist ploy: they put it about that I had harassed them all night by knocking at their door. Just like in New York, where you can file a complaint for an "inappropriate look." If this was the case in Europe, all the French and Italians would be in prison. Unfortunately for them, not content with supporting the war in Iraq, they were almost as wide as they were high, like thirty per cent of their fellow citizens. It so happens that my love life is not yet so restricted as to lead to an interest in this type of 'young woman.'

It is true that I had never attended a course on "Preventing sexual harassment", which is obligatory before entering the University of California. [61] Before becoming a member of staff in a chemical pharmaceutical research laboratory, this French researcher had to memorise two hundred clauses which would protect him from the loss of his car, his house, his savings and all material possessions, should he be deemed guilty of harassment. Just looking at a woman in the street is considered sexual harassment. Humiliating naked prisoners in Baghdad or Guantanamo is not. That's just defending American values and democracy!

Not only do Americans have a limited knowledge of history, they are both ignorant of and even despise other cultures. The problem being that even the strategists, when they embark on wars in the name of democracy and freedom, hardly acknowledge the culture of the country that they wish to suppress. The rest is all too well-known. In Vietnam a poor population on bicycles routed the most sophisticated army in existence.

Libya, Somalia, Iraq all followed, before Afghanistan and then Pakistan's turn. Such blindness and ignorance is appalling. They still haven't understood that culture comes before technical know-how. Neither the napalm bombs, nor the drones, nor the nine hundred kilo bombs can change anything. Neither can the secret prisons of the Eastern countries or northern Africa, where my beautiful country, Morocco, has been tarred in this way.

Their notorious Messianism is an injunction for them to save the world, without questioning their values, which are the best in the world! They therefore cannot listen to other nations, still less accept their existence. As goes the saying in war, they act first and think later. Action first, principles later.

Perhaps we should take a look at their education system to understand this a little better. One of my guests had a Masters in Business Administration from Harvard University. An MBA from Harvard is something, or so it is said in elite circles. I mean those that fly first class.

- Have you got a specialist subject, I asked him.

- Yes, I'm qualified in Math.
- Well you couldn't have landed in a better place, I said to him. I am currently looking into the school of Pythagoras. It's fascinating. His marital life as much a his way of teaching.

I thought that once again I had been visited by serendipity: this gift of finding what or who you want by chance. As this often happened to me, I was not really surprised. Alas, the poor man had never heard tell of a Pythagoras!

- So they don't teach you the history of Mathematics at Harvard?
- No, we just do Math, that's all. And that's what I love.

Here we were once again: action first, culture later, perhaps. Then I asked him what life was like at Harvard.

- Well, I'll tell you something that won't surprise you, nor please you.

Before we get there they send us a little Student's Guide, which says, among other things, that you may not bring:

- A guitar
- Literary works
- History books.

You will have better things to do, says the guide.

Then he continued:

- They teach you how to become the best, whilst maintaining a semblance of morality, even philanthropy.

As I said before, it's not attending a great school that matters; what's more worrying is getting into one.

Here's some good news from the United States: the death penalty has just been abolished in some states. Not for moral reasons, but financial ones. Let's take the practical side of things first. They are going to save over two million dollars. In France, there is an association of MPs who are fighting to bring back the death penalty. Their president is also honorary president for the Society for the Protection of Animals, the journalist tells us, with a touch of black… humour!

The election of a black President at the White House is definitely good news and a perceptible evolution in American society. However…
Here's what I heard on the local radio station: an Irish journalist was questioning the Primary electorate at the Democratic Convention:

- Are you going to vote for the black candidate?
- Me, vote for a black person? Don't imagine I will! But I'll have to, because the other choice is a woman!

The new black President seems perfectly clear in his intentions and his desire to converse with other nations and especially to listen to them. This will be a first in American history. He can get his country out of the trouble that his predecessor got it into by taking it down a dead end street. He is a brilliant character who has one great advantage: that of having lived abroad. This advantage allows him to have a more open mind than the majority of his fellow citizens, of whom only five per cent own a passport and have ventured beyond their state borders. However, I think it will be difficult to change the mentality of three hundred million individuals who cling to values which have long since become outdated. How could it be otherwise when six senators out of a hundred agree to closing Guantanamo, the other ninety-four refusing to do so. Or else, when the electorate for the deceased Senator Kennedy, did an about-turn and elected a Republican who supported torture – a chameleon never changes its skin. Mass has been said. On the other hand, this hasn't stopped him from continuing to drop bombs on innocent people in Afghanistan. He already was american, now he is just going to become more so.

A great philosopher has stated: “To be anti-American is to be anti-Semitic.” Here’s a profound thought. This great philosopher is French and calls himself “new”. Is there such a thing as a new philosopher? Too busy posing for magazines, he hasn’t had time to read Apollinaire. If he calls himself new, then he is too modest, since he has been known for a very long time, he whom the whole world is eager to listen to. In fact, didn’t Epictetus say of him: “Don’t be guilty of inferring ugliness to philosophy. Why cheat over such important issues? Why this lack of scruples? Why engage in something which doesn’t concern you? Cheat and do what you do. For this is what suits you best.” [62]

Marcus-Aurelius gave him counsel too:

“The way to live through philosophy is simple and conscientious; do not push it to vanity.” [63]

So, to be anti-American is to be anti-Semitic. This great thinker must be right. This must be the reason why Charlie Chaplin, left the United States without ever wanting to return. It wasn’t because he was suspected of sympathising with the Communists by McCarthy. During a stay in Paris he had an amusing way of making fun of Americans: “I am honoured that my work has been so appreciated by French people for so long. I think you have understood my heart and my instinctive sense of beauty. I say that because in all the nuances that I have included in my films, it was always with the aim of saying, as I have always said to my assistant, the French will understand that.”

This was an elegant way of saying that the Americans would never understand. Chaplin was supposedly anti-Semitic! The proof: he died on Christmas day.

To be anti-American, is to be anti-Semitic. This is doubtless why Franz Kafka, in his novel, *America*, is not overly-kind towards this country. It is true that he was inspired by Holitscher: "You can buy art, but not produce it." Kafka must have been anti-Semitic. The proof: he never went to America!

To be anti-American is to be anti-Semitic. Serge Prokofiev had to leave New York because he wasn't given the position which had been promised to him. Prokofiev was supposedly anti-Semitic. The proof: he composed the *Overture on Hebrew Themes*.

To be anti-American is to be anti-Semitic. Mahler was director of the Metropolitan Opera. Mahler was supposedly anti-Semitic. The proof: his post as director of the opera was withdrawn.

To be anti-American is to be anti-Semitic. Harold Pinter wrote: "The crimes of the USA across the world have been systematic, constant, clinical, without remorse and perfectly documented, but nobody speaks about them. They have supported, helped and often brought about all the military dictatorships of the right in the world since 1945!" [64] Pinter was supposedly anti-Semitic. The proof: he was one of the greatest playwrights of the twentieth century.

To be anti-American is to be anti-Semitic. The great Polish pianist, Krystian Zimerman, has just stated at the end of his concert in Los Angeles, that he will never again set foot in the United States, as a protest against the military policy of Washington: Guantamano and the missiles in Poland. Some members of the audience insulted him. Zimerman is supposedly anti-Semitic. The proof: the U.S. customs destroyed his piano; it had a strange smell.

To be anti-American is to be anti-Semitic. Sigmund Freud, being obliged to leave Vienna ahead of the Nazi putsch, refused to settle in the United States. "People are too materialistic, with their naive faith in the power of the dollar." He felt horrified. He wrote to his daughter, Mathilde, after leaving this country where he had given a few lectures: "I'm so glad to have left, and even happier that I won't have to live in such a country." Again: "The country and its citizens are hypocritical, uneducated, superficial, and love only money." "It's the anti-Paradise," he would say to Arnold Zweig. Centered on efficiency, "they have no time for their libido," he wrote to Jung. And "always in a hurry, reaching a high degree of culture would be impossible for them." Of psychoanalysis: "It always seemed to me that analysis suited the Americans like a white shirt on a crow" And, "When not naive and prudish, they are cunning, greedy and conventional." Freud was supposedly anti-Semitic. The proof: he spoke about sexuality. [65]

I'll stop my quotations of Freud here, for throughout his long life, he produced worse which I dare not repeat here, not out of prudishness but I simply do not want to add any more. On the other hand, faced with this catalogue, I understand better why our own Joker loves this country. As for psychoanalysis, Freud's prognosis turned out to be spot on: in America psychoanalysis has been converted to behaviourism, meaning the control of behaviour, the aim of which is to resolve both practical and emotional problems. Learning to suppress anxiety by helping the patient to adapt to his environment. It's the environment that counts, not the patient... Which is to confuse what is said about something with what one says. By placing the cure first and foremost other values are substituted in place of one's desire. It allows one to survive, but I myself am interested in living. Thank you Mr Freud. Thanks to you, I am living. And I haven't finished with clearing all the debris away or with living! Without bothering myself with behaviourists and neuroscientists (they really exist).

As for that great new philosopher, he is better known for the handful of chest hair that is trying to escape through his half-open shirt, in short, for his chest rather than his treasure. It seems that there are still people who buy his books, but I'm not sure.

Since we are on the subject – what is Judaism? Who are the Semites? For me the Jewish people can be summed up in two sentences:

"Jehovah gave Israel to Abraham: all the country that you see, I will give it to you and hence to your people for evermore." [66]

"Abraham is going to become a big and powerful nation, for I have chosen him so that he may order his sons and his house to keep the way of Jehovah." [67]

Therefore, God gave the land of Israel to Abraham and his people. And Abraham's people were chosen by God. But if you do not believe in God, like me, what does all this mean? The Jewish people are an ethnic group united by a religion which has lasted for centuries. Why have the Jewish people endured through centuries where other ethnic groups have disappeared, and other religions have been crushed by history, wars and conquests. If it has held fast, then it is precisely because they are sure that they are the chosen race. This certainty can be destroyed by nothing, neither pogroms, deportation, Nazism nor death. "Our enemies might well attack our bodies, but they can do nothing to wound our souls, because we are the chosen race. Whatever our sufferings, they do not prevent us from seeing God. He is waiting for us, we are his children." In this respect they are like the Christian martyrs who are happy to be reunited with God. As was said by one ecclesiastic on his death-bed: "I am content to die for this evening I will dine with Jesus." "I'm fine, I'm not too hungry," replied his friend. The difference, in my opinion, is that the Christian martyr is an individual. The martyr has been chosen by God to endure what must be endured. "I wear my cross, it's my fate," he would say; "Didn't Christ suffer in order to save mankind?" It is the same for a religious vocation: it is responding to a call which is both personal and individual.

Whereas in the Jewish religion, it is the entire people that are chosen. The individual does not question it. He is part of the chosen race. Full stop. There is no place for doubt. Which is what gives him his self-assurance which has defied time, for which they have at times been reproached, witness General de Gaulle's remark: "A race of the elites, self-assured and dominating." [68]

In everyday life, we come across this sensation when faced with someone who is a little too sure of themselves, whether it is the office, in an administrative context, or even while driving a car, or on board a plane when the hostess is a little too directive. If we don't say it, we often think it: "who does s/he think s/he is!" It is this grain of elitism, even when it is implicit, which can be seen in this race who call themselves the chosen ones (*elite* comes from 'elected', 'chosen'). This impression can also be found amongst aristocrats who add arrogance.

Pythagoras said: "May the behaviour of an aristocrat never cause you to despise." I'm not talking about snobs (*sine nobilitas*) who, having no nobility, are content with stupidity. Like the young woman who was so typical of the 16th quarter in Paris and who came with me one day to do some shopping for the group of friends who had come to a little village in the Anjou region to spend the week-end. Asking the grocer for ten litres of his best wine, I corrected myself when I remembered that the owner of the property had asked me to take two extra litres for the workers who were doing some building work in his house:

- You can put in two extra litres, I said to the grocer.
- But you're not going to take the best wine for the workers! exclaimed the woman who had accompanied me.

Yes, they still exist! It seems that there are still people who vote for the right!

Read in the newspaper: golden youth has just declared "the economic crisis, we're just laughing at it."

Marie-Antoinette also laughed...

The other side of Jewish people is their attachment to religion and its traditions. This cultural aspect has allowed them to move through one century to another, from one country to another, without ever losing their sense of identity, generation after generation. In Spain the Marranos are a good example of this: forced to convert to Christianity, they secretly kept their faith. This is why the Diaspora remains so strong. They are never completely absorbed by the culture of their host country. They are completely resistant to total integration. From New York to the most far-flung valley of the High Atlas, Jewish communities remain Jewish. During one of my visits to southern Morocco, a Berber told me that an American Jewish banker had come on a pilgrimage to the place where he was born and where his family had lived for centuries, before the Arabs arrived! To my question: "Has the conflict with Israel made things difficult between you?" he replied "Not at all, he was born here, so he's Moroccan. Like you, you're French, but you're on home ground here. It's your country since you were born here. On the other hand the first advisor of the king is Jewish. And Mohamed V protected the Jews during the war, which earned him the title of 'Compagnon of the Libération' by General de Gaulle." "Tell me one other thing, the Berbers represent seventy per cent of the Moroccan population, why don't they take power?" "It's very simple: because they already have! From the mayor of Casablanca to numerous ministers, they're all Berbers."

The Jewish people have always maintained their individuality, which has been more or less respected depending on their host country. The legendary tolerance of this Muslim country has been even greater than that of many other countries. And I'm not just thinking of Isabelle the Catholic!

I'll leave the last word to Albert Einstein, since I share his opinion when he wrote: "For me, the Jewish religion, like all religions, is an incarnation of the most infantile superstitions. And the Jewish people in which I am happily included, and for whom I share a profound affinity in their outlook, is no different, for me, to any other race. From my own experience they are no better than other groups of humans, even though they have been protected from the worst of cancers by their lack of power. In other words, I can see nothing 'chosen' about them." [69]

These are the thoughts of the man who declined the motion to become Israel's second president.

This brings us to the link between American Jews and Israel. A lot is said of the Jewish lobby in the United States. This is not quite correct, since the most important lobby is the AIPAC, which is a pro-Israeli lobby of some standing and with which a large number of Jewish people do not identify. On the other hand, it includes at its heart a great number of Christian fundamentalists, who are also called Christian Zionists and who have an idealistic vision of the Bible. The pro-Israeli lobby is not a Jewish lobby. It's an alliance between the Zionist Christians and Jewish

Zionists, so that the biblical prophesies can be achieved through the complete occupation of Palestine and the return of all Jews from the Diaspora.

But in order for the Messiah to return, the Jews must first be converted. Those who will not do so will be exterminated at Armageddon "in a great quake, the like of which has never been seen since the dawn of mankind" [70] Therefore, in this adventure, it is the Jews who will be the dupes in the whole affair. Their elimination will be the condition for the return of Christ. But this is far from being the case; the Jews know very well that it's all a farce and they're not the dupes in this story.

The support of the fifty million American Christian Zionists serve their interests in the short and medium term, for the Israeli national Zionists are hardly worried about the Apocalypse and the myth, for what they want is to live now as a people who are part of current history. This is why real anti-Semites are Christian Zionists, who support Israel in order, eventually, to destroy the Jews and Judaism as a religion, so that their prophesy can come true. Strengthened by this support, the State of Israel can allow itself to indulge in excessive aggression towards Libya or Gaza, knowing that the Americans won't move, since the United States government does not want to cut itself off from its Christian Fundamentalist and pro-Israel electorate.

This certainty of being within one's rights, in the name of the religion which one interprets accordingly, allows for all manner of bloody wrong-doings. And this is nothing new. Already in 1209 during the siege of Béziers, the Pope's representative issued to the Cathars who were trapped in the church of Sainte-Marie Madeleine, the famous words: "Kill them all, God will recognize his own." This sentence has, from time to time, been contested by historians. It is true that all those who heard it form part of the seven thousand dead simply left where they lay!

The Spanish clergy did the same thing in Latin America. The protestant pastors in Australia were no better.

Religions, how many crimes have been committed in the name of their Gods. That of Socrates, who believed only in his own dictum, that is to say his “demon”. Or that of Christ, who only believed in himself. But I am just battering down an open door. So I’ll close it once more.

We were celebrating the arrival of Spring which takes place on the first of February, Saint Brigid's day, according to the Celtic calendar, which is a lot more logical than our own, since it maintains the middle of the summer on the 21st of June, the longest day of the year. Through the night we were all gathered in the little pub, making the famous Saint Brigid crosses with rushes cut during that afternoon. These crosses would then join all the other religious regalia and images which decorate the majority of Irish homes. But before this they will have been blessed by the priest who goes from pub to pub in order to do so. It is true that the first time this happened I was surprised to see everyone fall to their knees. I had not seen the priest enter and prepare to make the blessing. The evening ended in Guinness-strength style. The priest and Sean, the local bank manager were not the last to toast Saint Brigid, who is also an Irish patron saint.

The next day was more difficult. Sean managed to get to his office where he saw a farmer who had come to borrow money to buy a new tractor:

- Still suffering from a terrible head, I could hardly follow all the explanations he was giving me and his reasons for needing a new tractor, so I fell asleep, my head falling onto the desk.

The farmer ran out of my office, shouting for assistance:

- Come quick, the manager is dead! He's had a heart attack!

It all ended in the pub where the manager was revived. I never knew if the farmer got his loan.

One rainy Sunday afternoon I was repainting my kitchen whilst moaning to myself: "If I was a bank manager I could at least pay someone to do this job." This idea was sufficient excuse for me to put down my brush in the middle of the job and pay a visit to my friend Sean, the bank manager. His smiling wife opened the door.

- Sean isn't in? I said downheartedly, still smelling of white spirit.
- Yes, yes he's here. He's repainting the kitchen. I've been asking him for weeks and he's finally got down to it!

It's no good envying your pals.

Sign of the times: the medics parties are no longer held in the hospital wards, I'm told. I have such good memories of them, thanks to my medical student friends.

Another sign of the times: the car manufacturers are no longer very inventive, they copy cars from fifty years ago: the Fiat 500, the Volkswagen Beetle, the Morris mini, the Citroën DS.

Even the Left is no longer what it was. Having started the war in Algeria, and having introduced Disneyland to Paris, they pass the first anti-libertarian laws banning smoking, create Paris-plage and are surprised to find that they no longer represent the spirit of freedom and culture to which people on the Left aspire. Leave that to your opponents, they love it. And don't forget the Tahitian proverb: "When you want to climb up the mast, make sure your bottom is clean!"

You may have noticed that my master remains the mayor of Bordeaux who, in the 16th century, was a friend of La Boetie's. I have however spared you the Latin quotations and kidney stones giving way to ill-tempered outbursts with which he peppers his Essays. My own stones only lasted one summer, spent on the beach without water in the company of a *cailín*. Her mother called me "the one who is going to die." I was twenty years old. I was already free from fearing or hoping for anything. I still am. What I know today I have always known. I have simply learned to express it and to live it fully. The idea of retiring has never even crossed my mind.

I was stuck in a Paris traffic jam in a taxi. I said to the driver:

- You're not sick of going nowhere in a traffic jam?
- Not at all. I'll tell you something: I retired two years ago. My wife had a little house in the Philippines, by the sea, so we went over there. After six months we'd had enough lolling about the beach at our age. We came back to Paris and I sat behind the wheel of my taxi once again. I am constantly amazed by the sight of people in their cars, making a little friendly wave to them here and there. I don't feel stressed or rushed. Every morning I savour life.

It's sometimes useful to live out our imaginary dreams. But you still have to be able to come back from them!

I often heard people say: "I'll do this or that when I retire." I always replied: "No, do it now." You shouldn't wait for what you really desire. I wouldn't want to find myself on my death-bed regretting that I hadn't tried to do what I wanted to do, even if it didn't work out - which hasn't been the case up until now.

I studied philosophy against the wishes of my father. And I was able to respond to my own desire. I did it without feeling guilty and without betraying my vision of life. And that sublimation is the very savouring of life. It is definitely not the possession of worldly goods. There are two titles of literary works of which I'm envious: *For how much longer can we Put off the Inevitable,* (in *The Time of the Assassins*) by Henry Miller and Raphaële Billetdoux' '*Mes nuits sont plus belles que vos jours* (My nights are lovelier than your days). Even though I have not been able to use these titles, I have included something of them in my life.

If at times I tend to forget them or push them away, my old demon comes back like a boomerang to remind me, even more forcefully for having tried to restrain them. I will always be a black sheep. And since I have accepted this demon, and know what it entails, I do not shrink from it. At times it causes a few ripples, but I take full responsibility for them. Sometimes I sublimate him and this is the ultimate high.

The Irish have understood this perfectly well, or at least those who are glad to see the present economic crisis: "It'll bring us back to what really matters. All this buying cars, gadgets, toys, was getting ridiculous." So I've told them about my new plan :

- I'm going to buy fifty donkeys and sell them to the owners of German saloons. Then they can continue to roll by as they wave to the crowds, seated in their limousines pulled by donkeys.

Only the ad men are confident. "We have to bear the load during the recession, then we'll use some marketing to get them to buy things they don't need again," as the head of a large advertising company said recently!

When I was running my book shop, I asked my musical clients, musicians, journalists, what in their opinion, would be the best machine for listening to music. They all replied in the same way: "I've only got a wonky old thing, that's not what's important!" It was only the successful forty-year old executives who had the really sophisticated equipment.

An Italian woman who arrived at my hideaway, overwhelmed by its charm, said *senza vergogna*:

- Are you God?

- How did you know? Was the only fitting reply.
No, as soon as you do something a little different, you are taken for someone extraordinary, which is obviously ridiculous. Having said this, I cannot prove that I am not God, since he does not exist. On the other hand I can prove that I am neither Thales, Pythagoras, Socrates, Epictetus, Jesus, the Buddha, nor Mohammed, since I have been obliged to write these few chapters myself. This doesn't give you the right to judge me since those who judged Socrates committed suicide and Judas, who allowed the condemnation of Christ, did likewise, it is said.

Being afraid of judges bothers me no more than being afraid of the police. Here they're so agreeable that everyone respects them. Except for the other day. Plastic cones had been placed along the main thoroughfare to prevent people from parking during the day. Our good friend Pat was there in his fine uniform. A car stopped right in front of him and the driver got out and moved the cone onto the pavement so that he could park. Pat looked at me with a wide smile of resignation and said :
- What can I do?

I am sitting here in my study writing these lines, here in my dungeon which overlooks the ocean on the one side and the hills on the other, the four windows giving me an uninterrupted three hundred and sixty degree view. I think back to the lighthouse of which I wanted to be the keeper when I was twenty years old. After making a few enquiries at the naval and sea ministry, I changed my mind when I found out that there were two keepers to every lighthouse who took the work in turns. My dreams of literary solitude evaporated. I don't regret it. I do not watch over the sea, it is she, my mother who now watches over me from the tree which looks down on my cottage. I don't look out for the ships in the distance; I look after my guests who lie sleeping just below me.

On more than one occasion I provided a resting place for deep sea captains. One evening I watched over the captain of the Queen Mary II. Like Themistocles' son, I imagined myself responsible for thousands of passengers…

One November night there was another deep sea captain of a merchant navy vessel who was trying to find some rest. It was a rough, rainy, windy, stormy night. He was sleeping in the little cottage with a thatched roof where arched ceiling joists add to the cosy charm of this little thick-walled room.
The next morning he came in to breakfast confessing that:

- Paul, this windy night made me dream I was on my ship and that the storm was about to sink us. I woke up with a start and found myself in a huge wine barrel. How happy I was!
- I know, I replied, sleeping in that room is every alcoholic's dream…

An ambassador from a European country confided in me that he was feeling anxious because in six months' time he would be retiring. I really don't know what I am going to do. He asked me about my book shop, wondering whether that wouldn't be an option. The idea of finding himself without having to attend receptions, without his chauffeur, without any title, was unbearable for him. I tried to reassure him, but I found it difficult. When you only exist through your function, it is difficult to be yourself.

I have always been interested in the different paths of the people I meet in my home or of those in biographies that I have read. I'm thinking for example of Scott Peck, [71] the author of numerous works full of the wisdom of life and self discipline, giving his married life of forty-three years as an example. Then, after an infidelity which he refers to as "a brief visit to God's castle", his wife left him and his children refused to see him. He continued to live like a prophet, without being a saint, he says. Then alcohol and tobacco ended his life. He had only one regret, he maintained, towards the end: not having drunk and smoked enough... Wisdom or religion can provide an alibi for filling up one's *crater*. When they are gone, one returns to the usual substitutes: tobacco and alcohol!

One's fate can be entirely dependant on a mother's wishes. The case of Romain Gary is a striking example. She wanted him to be a writer, and he was. She wanted him to become a diplomat, and he became one. She wanted him to become a hero of the Resistance, and he did. She didn't want him to know that she had died. He remained in ignorance. For three years after her death she had engaged a friend to post letters that she had written in advance. How does one get out of such a maternal lie, except by increasing one's efforts in order to exceed her post mortem wishes. He wrote even more. He won the Goncourt again. He increases his feminine conquests. But it was never enough to fill the *crater*, especially when it is not one's own. So, being no longer able to either find sexual fulfillment or to sublimate, he killed himself! He, who was so often given as an example of a well-filled life. But a life which is full can also be empty of meaning: one's own.

Filling one's life with success can be a form of failure. Denying one's own wishes is like denying life. It means forbidding one's own demon from revealing itself. This demon can take the form of a black sheep who will assume the strength of his vision.

The most desirable position, the most prestigious qualification, the most beautiful wife, winning the Goncourt twice, or the most beautiful car, are all simply alibis for keeping the black sheep quiet, by parading him in a white coat which is simply like Nessus' tunic, as are the most sophisticated philosophical reasonings. Social success can become the fortress in which one's suffocated fantasies take refuge for fear of discovering what we always knew. Suppressing the outward signs of one's desire will not stop it from resurfacing in another form, for it is implacable, and in many cases it will be too late.

Pinned down by one's noteworthy qualifications and social success, all that remains is for oneself to become nailed by a cancerous onslaught. Refusing this yoke is to flaunt liberty as I am so often accused of doing, for I frequently step over the boundaries within which I am supposed to be confined. A terrible jealousy may ensue. I accept this.

Refusing to make concessions is not a sign of intolerance. It means first of all refusing to do what others want you to do. The "it's for your own good" must be banished if it does not correspond to what I am, what I think, what I know and what I feel. I would allow no-one to make me say or do something which is not me. I humbly recognise that it has taken me time to achieve this.

Charles Trenet said to Léo Ferré: "You'll never succeed because you don't want to make any concessions." Following the madness of one's vision is quite another thing to being a singing madman. At times fate takes its revenge: Ferré the anarchist died on the fourteenth of July. But before this he had written: "Mr Past, let me pass over." And "Happiness is sadness lying down for a rest."

The father of two young women thought he had landed the king pawn when one of his daughters married President Kennedy's son. A few years later the son in law led himself and the two daughters to their deaths in a plane crash. The father had hugely mistaken his destiny.

Fate may take another form. You simply have to believe in it:

My young son had gone on holiday with his mother and a book which he had borrowed from me. An hour after being airborne on the return flight he asked his mother:

- Did you pick up the book Dad lent me?
- No, you were reading it in the departure lounge.
- I'm going to be in trouble. It's really important to Dad.
- Don't think the plane is going to turn back just to get your book!
- Half an hour later, the captain announced:
- One of our reactors is on fire, fasten your seatbelts, I am going to empty the fuel tank and we are going back to land. Please remain calm, there shouldn't be any problems. There were no problems. He found my book in the departure lounge and, half an hour later in the second plane which took them back to Paris, my son said to his mother:
- You see, Mum, the plane went back to get my book! Teenagers are nearly always right!

As for myself, I lent a small torch to a young Australian couple so that they could find their way when they came back to the cottage on foot late at night. Five years later I received a little parcel from Australia with the following note:

- We borrowed this from you five years ago when we were on our honeymoon. This torch is happy to be reunited with its rightful owner. It was hidden at the bottom of a drawer. Many apologies.

One should never lose hope!

Even though, as we grow older, hope starts to wane. However… I have just learnt a lesson from the Persian general, Mermeroes. At seventy-eight years of age, he distinguished himself among the heroes of the East by the wisdom of his counsel and his valour in battle: his age and infirmity, which meant he no longer had the use of his legs, did nothing to diminish his fighting spirit, nor his body. Carried on a bed stretcher to the front lines, he filled the enemy with terror and inspired valiant confidence in his troops who were always victorious when they fought beneath his flag. [72]

My friend Peter was helping me do some work at the cottage. He was eighty years of age. He was a 'stone master', a master in the art of building stone walls. Always smiling and in good humour, he climbed up onto the roof to secure the thatch; the height of the long ladder didn't bother him in the least. It was from this height that he spat on the next stone down below that he had selected to finish the wall. Young Vincent had to hoist up the desired object, marked by saliva, and get the thing up to Peter. He died at ninety years of age, in my arms, saying to me: "Paul, life is too long." I salute you, Peter, thank you for everything you have taught me.

I would also like to pay homage to the illustrator, Siné who, at eighty years of age, has just launched a new weekly journal. After fifty years spent combating human stupidity and all the *ayatollahs* of every colour, he still has the energy to defend smokers even though he is a non-smoker himself. I am extremely proud to be the first subscriber.

Thank you to all the eighty-year olds for everything they have taught us, even though Vercingétorix was just twenty at the battle of Alesia and died at twenty-six in Caesar's caves.

As for myself, I sail between the two and can't complain, as did a certain chestnut tree which must have been over a hundred years old. It was one evening in a sunny park in the South of England. Lying on the grass, young English girls in short skirts were fooling around.

The chestnut tree against which I was leaning murmured:

- When I was young, I only saw crinolines, it is only now when I am old that I see all these little bottoms presented to me.

I replied: "Lucidity, my dear, what have I done that you should thus imprison me."

Those that try to understand who they are, are often accused of navel-gazing. Yet this isn't as stupid as it seems. '*Nombril*' (navel) comes from *omphalos* which gave us *ombilic* (umbilical) and his cord: the *Omphalos* was the stone monument in the form of an egg which was situated at Delphi in the temple of Apollo. It was venerated as the centre of the world, famous for its prophecy of the Pythia who spouted incoherent words which the priests interpreted for the pilgrims. In the end it is just a roundabout way of becoming what we are. Not to be confused with '*sarcomphale*' which is cancer of the navel…. Nor with '*sarcophile*' which is a heavy animal with short legs which is also called the Tasmanian devil because of its extreme ugliness. [73] Nor with 'Sarkophants'. But that's another story. [74]

There is one other way and that is through dreams. Montaigne understood this well, before Freud came along: "Dreams are the faithful interpretations of our inclinations; but matching and understanding them is a real art." [75]

Epicharmus was not too far off either: "Dreaming is not dependent on free will, for how can the dreamer intervene in what he receives."

What we receive we already have. For example, I am a modest person and I will show off my modesty: my *cailín* had lent me her car to go to the station to catch the train to Paris. It was February and it was cold. I had just had an article with my picture, boasting the delights of my B&B, published in a Parisian weekly. In the evening, as I was returning by train, a passenger sitting opposite me was reading this journal. I waited for him to reach the page in question to hide my face as much as possible behind my hand. He read the whole article and then went on to the next page. I relaxed a little. He got out at the same station as myself. We made our way to the car park. His car was parked next to mine. Our windscreens were frozen over. We scraped away at them in unison. I said to myself: he must be dreaming of Ireland. He couldn't imagine that I might be standing just a couple of metres from him in the dead cold of night. I didn't want to destroy his dream and never made myself known.

I had been so shocked by an article which told the story of a union president for European managers, seeing the person seated next to him on a plane reading an article about him, gave him a nudge of the elbow saying: "You see that guy, it's me." [76]

The same thing happened to the author of *The Alchemist*. He was sitting on a café terrace when a mother passing in front of him said to her daughter: "You really should read *The Alchemist*." He got up, caught them up and said: "It's me, I am the author of *The Alchemist*." I've already told you, I must be too modest.

My modesty takes me to the end of this work. I was waiting for inspiration. I didn't know what I was going to write… Until I understood that not knowing, I might say it all the better. If I had known, I would only have written an exposé like we do at university. Inspiration does not come into it, only the exhalation of everything I wanted to say. If you haven't grasped the nuances of everything I've spelt out, then it really is of little importance. The important thing is that you felt something… The rest is literature…

Be on the lookout, all the same; the *ayatollahs* are still there. In the same way that the photograph of the portrait of the Saint Helena reclusive can be more powerful that the original painting, a paper photograph becomes more luminous and more real when it is digitally rendered and so the ayatollahs that abound these days in their three-piece suits can strike with more might than the real bearded *ayatollahs* in their *djellabas*! The copy can often be worse than the original.

Fortunately? Brassens is there and always tells the truth, even in *Histoire de faussaire* (The Story of a Forger) [77]

Stay on the lookout. The *ayatollahs* are like mountaineers: they are always there.

No doubt I have not written everything I wanted to say. But as I have said many things I did not want to write, I stand condemned!

I prefer to shape my life with my demon's chisel before my name is chiseled in stone. Should these few chapters be lost, forgotten in the jumble of history, I won't fall into a *post mortem* depression.

EPILOGUE

I was born in an Arab country in the middle of July, on the anniversary of the Hegira, which marks the beginning of the Muslim era. In a little village called Berrechid, which is also the first word of the Bible in Hebrew, and which means beginning. [78] Born of a mother who dreamt of becoming a Carmelite nun but finally chose to have children who would find God's vocation (it didn't work out). The only doctor in the area was a psychiatrist and this was the first man I set eyes upon when I came into this world. By being born I saved my father's life, at least this is what I like to think, since my arrival made him the father of five children, which allowed him to be demobbed. In Casablanca I lived in rue Dalou, named after a sculptor who played an active part in the Commune of Paris. [79]

The assistant mayor, a young greenhorn, presided over my marriage in France. No doubt in order to show off his knowledge of the Bible, when he read out the official marriage certificate, referred to me as Paul Berrechid. Everyone present burst out laughing. He then excused himself. It was perhaps the only time in his life that he made apologies, for since then a majority of naive French citizens, who themselves were cleverly manipulated, have granted him the reins of power.

In spite of this last handicap, life can still be beautiful.

NOTES

Page 9.

[1] First president of the Irish Republic.

Page 10.

[2] Niko Kazantzaki, *L'Odysée*, Plon, 1971.
James Joyce : *Ulysse*, Gallimard, 1929.
James Joyce, *Dedalus*, Gallimard 1943.
Georges Brassens, *Pénélope*, 1960.

Page 16.

[3] *Letter to Alma*, 27th June 1909

Page 21.

[4] Frank Harte, 'My name is Napoleon Bonaparte', Hummingbird records, 2000.

[5] *The Daily Telegraph*, 5th January 2002.

Page 22.

[6] Ursula Kubler.

Page 25.

[7] *Le Monde*, 11th September edition, dated 12th September 2003.

Page 28.

[8] Paul Chatenoud, 'An Irishman's Diary', *The Irish Times*, 9th July 2004.

Page 30.

[9] Montaigne.

Page 33.

[10] Medical Research Institute of New Zealand.

[11] Dr Stanley Zammit, Cardiff University.

Page 35.

[12] Victoria Coren, *The Observer*, 10th August, 2008.

Page 37.

[13] *The Guardian*, 24th November, 2006.

Page 38.

[14] Fabian Barthez, Simon Garner, David James, Socrates, captain of the Brasil football team and medical student, Giorgio de Luca, Shirley Strong, Olympic medalist. *The Guardian* : 'Puffing their Way to Glory', by Peta Bee,

Page 39.

[15] Smoking increased officially by 2,6 % in 2009. This fact confirms my analysis. That is to say, that during a period of crisis when people are more anxious than usual, the urge to seek some form of compensation in tobacco is quite logical. In reality the figure of 2,6 % is wide of the mark, for many smokers buy their cigarettes in neighbouring countries where the price of cigarettes is lower, and where the black market has never been so robust! (In Ireland I know of no-one who buys their cigarettes from the tobacconist.)
This illustrates yet again both the hypocrisy and the ridiculous nature of the anti-smoking laws.

Page 43.

[16] Frederick B Levensen, *Causes and Prevention of Cancer*, Sidgwick & Jackson, London, 1984.

Page 45.

[17] I'm going to be in a position to reduce the cost of my breakfast by leaving out the bacon. In fact, Professor Martin Wiseman (whose name befits him well), medical advisor to the World Cancer Fund, has just announced that by reducing one's consumption of bacon by seventy grams per week, the risk of cancer is considerably lower. Long live the evangelical vegetarian brigade!

Page 46.

[18] *The Guardian*, 12th February, 2009.

[19] "Plants can grow proteins – which is what antibodies are – and if they're genetically modified, they can grow specific proteins that scientists know will act on

the HIV virus." The process is already being carried out in the Fraunhofer Institute for Molecular Biology and Applied Ecology in Germany. *The Guardian*, 2nd February 2010.

Page 48.

[20] "The Ladies' Walk", famous battleground during the Great War.

Page 60.

[21] See Maupassant's *Un Portrait*.

Page 65.

[22] Hippocrates, *Complete Works*, 1934.

[23] " (…) his first extravagant holidays in New England where he is to meet George Bush this weekend, and was seen jogging in a T-shirt with the slogan 'I am an American agent' (…) He is not embarrassed to flaunt his expensive tastes and rich friends but rather seeks to legitimise them in line with celebrity spectacle." Paul Gillespie, World editor, *Irish Times*, 11th August 2007.

[24] "Why has a people as style-conscious as the French elected someone who is such a loser? (…) a man whose superficial inadequacies are risible. (…) The French elected a man who can't see that he doesn't look silly because he is short; he looks silly because he is standing on a box. Maybe he should think about retraining as an airline pilot or a surfing instructor? He definitely needs a sports car. (…) The French are rehabilitating the comical." David Mitchell, *The Observer*, (2nd August 2009)
Also see, regarding the *Joker* : www.thegreengate.eu – click on WHAT IT IS, then on 'Rigolo false cowboy.'

Page 79.

[25] Montaigne, *Essays*, Book III, Chapter V.

[26] Montaigne, *Essays*, Book III, Chapter XIII.

[27] Diogenes, *Life of Socrates*, II.

Page 81.

[28] Charles Fourier (1772-1837), theory of pivotal love.

Page 105.

[29] A well-intentioned reader informed me, doubtless because of her extensive knowledge on the subject of foreskins, that the 'real' foreskin of Christ was to be found at Charroux (in the Vienne department) in Poitou, where barren women used to make their pilgrimage in the Middle ages. It is in Chartres, before the 'real' veil of the Virgin that pilgrims go to pray (Her sources are : *La vie des femmes au Moyen Age*, by Sophie Cassagues. Ouest France pub)

[30] Saint Catherine of Sienna, 1347-1380.

[31] See the Ecstasy of Saint Theresa of Avila, one of Christ's other wives, notably in Gianlorenzo Bernini's sculpture in the Church of Santa Maria della Vittoria, Rome.

Page 110.

[32] Mac-Mahon, President of the French Republic, 1873-1879, was of Irish origin.

Page 121.

[33] *The Guardian*, 17th September, 2008.

[34] Speech at the Congress for Gynaecological Obstetricians.

Page 122.

[35] *The Irish Times*, 21st March, 2001.

Page 127.

[36] Henri Favre, 1882-1984, who flew the first seaplane in 1911.

Page 129.

[37] Aragon, *Le Fou d'Elsa*.

Page 130.

[38] Albert Einstein, *letter to the philosopher Eric Gutkin,* 3rd january,1954.

[39] Some readers have conveyed their disagreement when, paraphrasing Camus, I say that I prefer an ordinary Muslim to a Christian fundamentalist. Having lived in a Muslim country, I stand by my choice.

There is one person at least who will agree with me : Terry Holbrooks, the US Army soldier, warden of the inmates at Guantanamo. Fascinated by the calm composure of those prisoners who endured torture (recommended by the born-again Christian president), he converted to Islam : "I apparently had all the freedom that they did not have, but in fact, they were freer than I since they had freedom of thought, they were independent. As for me, I was a slave of the US Army."

Jean-Paul Sartre would not say otherwise : "I had never felt as free as when I was a prisoner in Germany."

As for myself, I practised this freedom of thought during the twenty-six months of my military service : deprived of physical freedom, and by definition material and social conditions, I was able to be entirely present within myself, without worrying about the mechanism which surrounded me and which had no effect on me whatsoever.

Having never endured torture, I have not felt the need to convert to Islam, nor any other religion : the free spirit is ample substitute for me. This is what I have tried to illustrate in my book.

Page 131.

[40] Montaigne, *Essays*, Book III, Chapter V.

[41]. Montaigne, *Essays*, Book III, Chapter V.

[42]. Sean O' Casey, *Inishfallen, Fare Thee Well*, 1949.

[43]. Brendan Behan, *Confessions of an Irish Rebel,* 1965.

Page 132.

[44] *The Irish Times*, 9th March, 2000.

Page 133.

[45] One of Bill Clinton's more outspoken critics concerning the affair with Monica Lewinsky and who voted for his impeachment, was Mark Sanford, Governor for South Carolina and President of the Republican Governors. He has just been exposed in his e-mails (there is sometimes sense in Big Brother) boasting the erotic beauty of his mistress's hips. We are pleased to learn that his wife

Jenny is finding comfort in reading the Psalms, and he himself in the Bible! The ayatollah's religion has some good in it : they fall into their own traps.
As was the case with the British minister who has just passed a new law restricting the amount of alcohol to be consumed by drivers and was found completely drunk at the wheel of his car two days after his law had been passed. Perhaps he wanted to celebrate the introduction of this legislation…

[46] Freud, *Dora.*

Page 140.

[47] Epictetus, *The Discourses*, Book IV.

Page 142.

[48] Philip O' Connor, *Memoirs of a Public Baby.* Faber 1958.

[49] Andrew Barrow, *Quentin and Philip, a double portrait,* Macmillan, 2002.

Page 146.

[50] Plutarch, *Life of Pericles.*

[51] *cynic* (Greek – 'dog')

[52] Epictetus, *The Discourses*, Book IV. Although he was a Stoic, he was very close to the Cynics.

Page 149.

[53] Alfred de Musset.

Page 159.

[54] "Paul Chatenoud was one of my philosophy students at the Sorbonne. Since my life is divided between philosophy and music; I am delighted to see the opening of a shop devoted to books on music and which is situated almost on my very doorstep, in the shadow of Notre-Dame itself. I sense that I will be a frequent browser along the shelves of this place, which I wish every success and the best of luck." Vladimir Jankélévitch.

[55] "Print runs of books on music are always limited. When a book is out of print, when one has lost all hope of finding it, you have only to push open the door to

Paul Chatenoud's, to find this musicologist and miracle maker." Alain Resnais.

Page 166.

[56] *Democracy in America*, Alexis de Tocqueville.

[57] *Democracy in America*, Alexis de Tocqueville.

Page 167.

[58] Geoff Hill, *The Way To Go*, Blackstaff Press,

[59] The Irish Times, Wednesday, may 22, 2002

Page 168.

[60] *The Guardian*, 16th July 2008

Page 169.

[61] See the article by Alexandre Lacroix, *Philosophie Magazine*, November 2008.

Page 173.

[62] Epictetus, *The Discourses*.

[63] Marcus Aurelius, *Reflections*.

Page 174.

[64] Harold Pinter's letter to Tony Blair, 1997.

Page 175.

[65] Some people accuse me of outright anti-Americanism. This would place me on an equal footing with Sigmund Freud, Charlie Chaplin or Harold Pinter. I accept the homage, even though it's as ridiculous as the accusation.

Page 176.

[66] *Genesis*, XIII, 14.

[67] *Genesis*, XVIII, 16.

Page 177.

[68] De Gaulle in 1967: "After the second World War, the founding of the State of Israel gave rise to some apprehension. One might well ask, in fact, and indeed a number of Jewish people have wondered, whether the implantation of this community on land which had been acquired under such circumstances, more or less justifiably, and in the midst of the Arab people who

are so opposed to them, would not lead to interminable friction and conflict. Some even doubted that the Jewish people themselves, who until now have been so dispersed, would not remain what they had always been; that is to say an elite race, rulers and sure of themselves, who, once they had reunited themselves on the site of their former splendour, wouldn't succeed in transforming the moving wishes that they have harboured over nineteen centuries, into a burning and conquering ambition: next year in Jerusalem." Charles de Gaulle, 1967.

Page 179.

[69] Albert Einstein, *Letter to the Philosopher Eric Gutkin*, 3rd January, 1954.

Page 180.

[70] *Revelation of Saint John*, Chapter XVI, 17-21.

Page 188.

[71] Scott Peck, *The Road Less Travelled*, 1978.

Page 192.

[72] War of the Colchos between Justinian and Chosroes, 549-556, Gibbon, *The Fall of the Roman Empire*.

Page 193.

[73] *Larousse universel* – 2 volumes, 1949.

[74] (…) It is hard to keep a level head when you are surrounded by sycophants. Or perhaps we should say Sarkophants. Fawning politicians and journalists could yet be the downfall of Nicolas Sarkozy. (…) This banana republic-style barrage has alas become de rigueur since his election. Lara Marlowe, *Irish Times*, 24th August 2007.

[75] Montaigne, *Essays*, Book III, Chapter XIII.

Page 194.

[76] *Le Canard Enchainé*, 14th March, 2001.

Page 195.

[77] Georges Brassens, *Histoire de faussaire* (Story of a Forger)

Page 196.

[78] This place of birth gave me the conquest of a few Jewish *cailins: "You are my beginning,"* they would say to me.

[79] Jules Dalou, 1832-1902, creator of Triomphe de la République, Place de la Nation in Paris, and of Victor Noir's *Gisant* in the Père-Lachaise cemetery. "The loin cloth of the recumbent figure is filled out by a swollen member. For hundreds of years young women have furtively caressed this protuberance which, being so cleaned and polished, shines with all its might. A homage to fecundity and the glory of love, this gesture bestows fertility or favour on those whom we desire." Francis Marmande in *Le Monde*, October 2003.

ISBN : 978-2-915459-32-6
EAN : 9782915459326
Dépôt légal : mai 2010
www.lescygnes.fr
Contacts : edicygne@free.fr
editionlescygnes@gmail.com
www.theeyeoftheventriloquist.eu (in English)
www.leregardduventriloque.eu (in French)

This edition printed May 2010
by Nouvelle Imprimerie Laballery
58500 Clamecy
Legal deposit : May 2010
Print n° : 005009

Printed in France

The Nouvelle Imprimerie Laballery has the "Imprim'Vert" mark